Making a Life

Twenty-Five Years of Hooking Rugs

BY DEANNE FITZPATRICK

NIMBUS
PUBLISHING
— NIMBUS.CA —

Nimbus Publishing Limited
3660 Strawberry Hill Street, Halifax, NS, B3K 5A9
(902) 455-4286 nimbus.ca

Printed and bound in Canada

NB1394

Cover and interior design: Kate Westphal, Graphic Detail Inc.
Editor: Emily MacKinnon
Proofreader: Paula Sarson

Library and Archives Canada Cataloguing in Publication

Title: Making a life : twenty-five years of hooking rugs / Deanne Fitzpatrick ; foreword by Sheree Fitch.
Names: Fitzpatrick, Deanne, author. | Fitch, Sheree, writer of foreword.
Identifiers: Canadiana 2018906854X | ISBN 9781771087230 (hardcover)
Subjects: LCSH: Fitzpatrick, Deanne. | LCSH: Textile artists—Canada—Biography. | LCSH: Rugs, Hooked.

Classification: LCC TT850 .F58 2019 | DDC 746.792—dc23

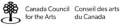

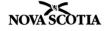

Canada   Canada Council for the Arts   Conseil des arts du Canada   NOVA SCOTIA

Nimbus Publishing acknowledges the financial support for its publishing activities from the Government of Canada, the Canada Council for the Arts, and from the Province of Nova Scotia. We are pleased to work in partnership with the Province of Nova Scotia to develop and promote our creative industries for the benefit of all Nova Scotians.

For seven sisters
and a childhood by the sea

TABLE OF CONTENTS

"Protecting the Young" (54 x 36, 2018). I like to use animals as symbols in my rugs. Here the two foxes face off against each other in a marriage, but remain undaunted. They protect the seven small foxes in the den.

FOREWORD

The first time I walked into Deanne Fitzpatrick's studio in Amherst, Nova Scotia, I felt I'd stepped over a threshold and entered a new world. Everything *shimmered*. As I looked around at the colours, inhaled the textures, and viewed the art on the walls all vibrating with such positive, powerful energy, I almost tasted those vivid colours, felt the swirls and designs of Spirit dancing. I was transported to a windswept road in rural Newfoundland with a tribe of women I somehow knew I belonged to. Sacred, magical worlds exist—and I knew I had discovered one. *Whoever this Deanne Fitzpatrick is*, I thought, *she "sees" beauty and love*. I wanted to be her best friend.

A few months later, I was lucky enough to meet her. I learned at once—and am still learning—that Deanne is a creative force, a goddess of woolcakes, an imaginative genius. She is a woman of faith. A wife, mother, entrepreneur, community leader, changemaker, homemaker, mentor, painter, visionary, artist, collaborator, retailer, radio host, elegant hostess, a voracious and literary reader. She has a flair for storytelling, as readers will discover in this book, and shares herself beautifully and meaningfully. She is a woman who works at the forefront in public, but just as often she is behind the scenes, simply "doing things" for people. Thoughtful things.

I'm not gushing; this is all true (although she'll blush when she reads this). Along with her huge heart, generous soul, intuition, and wellspring of boundless energy, Deanne is talented, modest, practical, and grounded. She's sensitive and stylish and combines all this with shrewd business acumen. She is, in a word, authentic. Her workshops bring in people from all over North America and beyond, and her art is found in private collections around the world. Her reach is far; her star is bright.

And I know all this to be true because she did become my friend. Not just a "best" friend, either, but something more: an *Anam Cara*—a soul friend. At the best of times she has been my muse, my illustrator, and my wise advisor in a new-to-me business venture. At the hardest of times she has been my lifeline, my listener, and my consoler. Did I mention she is funny?

So, I am biased. I love her like a sister and I admire her deeply. Readers will, too, as they discover the many facets of Deanne in the pages that follow—her passion, her knowledge of her art and its tradition. Above all else, readers will discover and appreciate Deanne's commitment to "create beauty every day," all while inspiring others to do the same.

Individually and collectively, through the act of creation, we can all make this world vibrate with the kind of beauty, art, and love Deanne brings to all she does.

To make art and to make a life. YES.

Every time I walk into her shops—two of them now—meet her for lunch, or chat on the phone, all these many years later, I still feel the world is ablaze with colours I have never seen before. More hopeful, more beautiful because of her.

Enter her world and be inspired.
—*Sheree Fitch*

"Where the Orchard Blooms" (48 x 64, 2018). I am always caught off guard by blooming orchards near an abandoned homestead. The story of how beauty remains long after everything is gone is so poignant.

INTRODUCTION

I make rugs. I am an artist. But I am not some kind of fancy artist the way I imagined artists might be when I was younger. I never went to art school, and I don't have a bunch of esoteric things to say about my rugs. When I was young I loved the idea of being "deep," but the older I get the more I love the idea of being accessible. In short, I am not a literary person; I am a practical person.

I am a maker of things, and these things are rugs. They are imbued with layers of meaning from fifty years gone by. They are thick with ideas and thoughts, but mostly they are about beauty. They are the story of my life.

I hooked before I had children. I hooked with babies on my knee. I hooked while I waited at home for teenagers on Saturday nights. I hooked my whole life away, and it has been sacred. I have gone to the frame as if I were on my knees in prayer. I have gone before it with humility, shame, and steeped in loss. It has always consoled me. It has always listened. I have also gone before it with glee, with hope and love. Most days I just go before it as if it were a practice, a habit. I go before it because it is my place. It's been a blessing that, at times, I had no understanding of.

A life of making. The making of a life.

I have lived a life at the altar of art. I have sacrificed time with my loves because of my own compulsion to create; it was never a choice, I just had to get to the frame. It still is that way. Though I know I should be "living," I often choose to sit alone and hook. Whatever regrets may bubble up later are not strong enough to change me. The frame is where I belong: it is my living; it sustains me; it nurtures me.

I am a woman who lives on seven acres, and I am at home amongst the brush and scrub. It is this place over twenty-five years ago, in fact the very house I live in now, that sent me to the mat in the first place. That old broken-down house with mud showing through the floors told me I needed to make mats. That house, that square of land in a quiet corner of northern Nova Scotia, told me what to do with my life, and I listened.

Thank God I listened, for I was young and barely knew *what* to listen to. There may have been signs all around, I don't know, but honestly, it seems that was the only one that was ever clear. That bit of land, that house, they spoke to me clearly and said, *I need mats for the floor.* These days I'm on the lookout for signs, but back then I was just twenty-four and living and not thinking too much. I did not have years of deciding things behind me.

I was *just* twenty-four, and I put a hook in my hand. To think of it now makes me weep. I knew that I would never put that hook down; I belonged to it and it belonged to me. I was blessed right there—anointed with something. I don't know what but it made me.

It made me whole.

It made me good.

It made me kinder.

Because I had found the thing to which I belonged. As I write this I have a lump in my throat. What if I had not listened? What if I had not known? Who or what would I be without this tool that has shaped my life?

I honestly have no idea because it is this making, this thrumming of the mat, which has rounded me out and given me the space to find and be myself.

A note regarding dates and measurements: I did my best to estimate the size (in inches) and date of these rugs, but they are approximations. It has been many years since most of these rugs have been in my studio.

"Queen Anne's Lace and Lavender" (42 x 42, 2018). I love that Queen Anne's lace is both abundant and delicate. It appears so fragile but thrives roadside in the plainest and dullest of conditions.

QUEEN ANNE'S LACE

When the light hits the Queen Anne's lace
that way,
the way you know is sudden and special,
it is time to stop
and breathe
and just
look.

It is the time to breathe in summer.
Fall on your knees and praise it, for nothing is
more deserving.

When beauty lays itself before you,
offered up,
simply and quietly,
it means to be taken in. It means to be loved.

That tiny plum centre of the filigree flower means
to be explored.
Touch it.
Trace it with your finger so you'll know in winter
what it felt like.

The walk might be the same every day,
but the light is never the same twice.
It filters and streams and casts shadows upon the
roadside.
It is a painter and means to be noticed.

The sky does not have a way of being
that makes you accustomed to it.
I have never said, "Oh, there it is again: the sky."
I have never tired of tilting my head towards it in
prayer,
in humility,
and seeing how small I really am;
reassured that I am part of something bigger.
Something so big that I cannot conceive or
imagine it,
even when I think my imagination is all big and
beautiful.

The sun rises every morning and transforms the
same
roadsides, fields, and shores that I passed
yesterday,
making me feel as if I have never gone down the
same road twice.
It heats up your back one day and chills your
fingers the next.
That is the power of light
as it shifts and paints
and makes me believe what I might have thought
impossible.
That what bored me yesterday has been touched
with frost,
become bronzed and weathered,
and is interesting to me again.
And then, once in a while, it shakes itself from its
leaves and becomes a silhouette
and snow falls all around it
and I am transfixed
until soon again, I wish for spring and buds
and life to emerge from the skeleton of winter on
the roadside.

ON MAKING RUGS

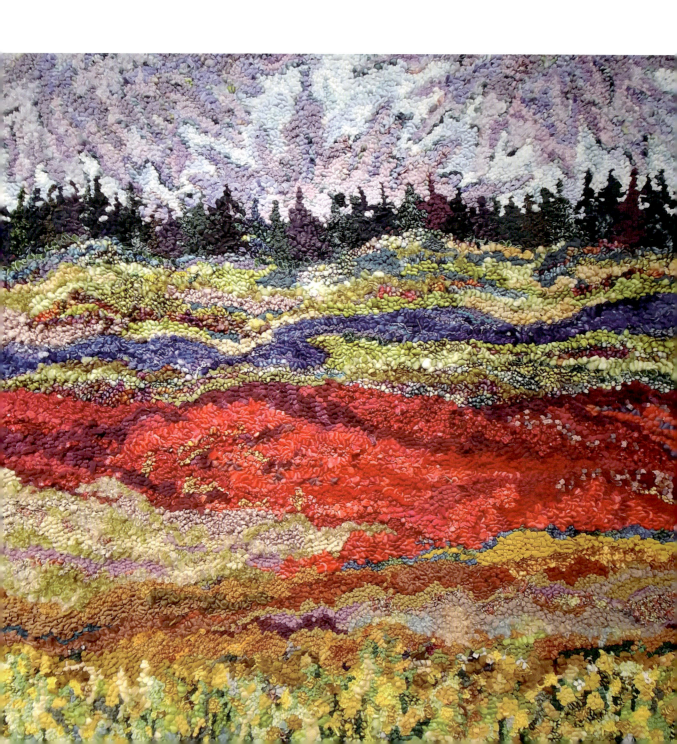

ACCIDENTAL ARTIST

I never imagined being an artist. As a child it sounded silly, and as I grew older it just sounded haughty. Honestly, it still sounds a little haughty to me after all these years. Art and rug-hooking were not part of my life growing up; they were both things I grew into. When I was about thirteen or fourteen, I was in a group called the CYC: the Catholic Youth Committee. It was a funny little group; a bunch of teenagers would meet in the town hall without any adults leading us. We just looked after ourselves and planned our own little events. Amazing really. We were left to our own devices. That would never happen today.

One weekend we put on a talent show, and one of my childhood friends and I were the actors. We had to dress up as men, sit at a table, and have a beer. Her line was, "What are you working at?" Mine was, "I am an artist."

Then she said, "An artist, an artist, you're not an artist!"

I replied, "I am, I am indeed."

She said, "Well if you are an artist what do you draw?"

And then I delivered the punchline: "I *am* an artist…I draws me unemployment."

This was rural Newfoundland in the late 1970s. We knew all about drawing

"Coastal Girls" (36 x 20, 2000). As the youngest of seven girls growing up by the sea, I feel like I belong on the coast. I have always watched women getting dressed to go out for the evening, the fun and joy it inspires in them.

< "The Golden Season" (46 x 48, 2018). The appearance of goldenrod , even in August, is sign of autumn. I watch the seasons here in Cumberland County, and for me they are marked by what is happening on the roadside.

unemployment and very little about drawing anything else.

There were no artists where I lived. The closest thing was Sister Sarah Beresford, the principal of our school, who used to walk out to the track by the local watershed to sketch and paint. Honestly, we all found it a bit odd. I remember people gossiping about it. But I also remember imagining what she was doing out there all alone on the track with her brushes and paints, and what her pictures might have looked like.

Sister Sarah was the first person I ever knew who made art of any kind. I was never friendly with her—she kept herself at a distance in her position as principal—but I did wonder about her. Sometime over the few years she was at our little Catholic school, she introduced art classes: they were held in a basement room with long tables and dark hardwood floors. I loved being in that basement with the dusty old floors and the late-afternoon sunlight floating down from the high windows. I loved the big, round, red pots of hardened watercolour paints and the endless reams of newsprint. To me it was one of the most beautiful places, that art room. I loved it there.

There in that basement was the first time I saw art supplies. Before that "art" to me was drawing in the extra pages of my father's

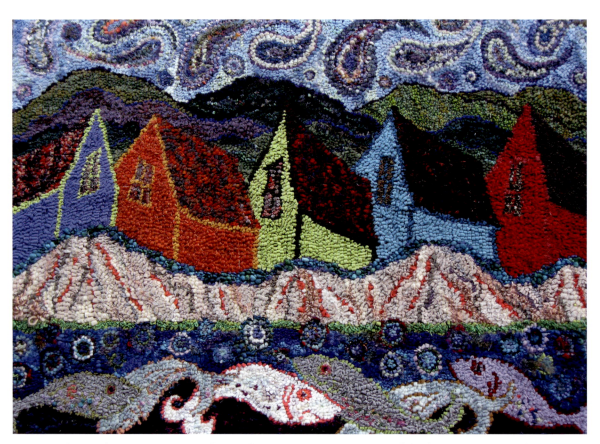

"From Sea to Sky" (48 x 42, 2002). This was hooked in 2010 and was one of the first times I added elements like paisley in the sky. Proudly, it has appeared in several high school social studies textbooks in Atlantic Canada.

"Mackerel Sky" (24 x 24, 2016). The fish is laid before the house because it was sustenance in most Newfoundland homes when I grew up. I like a red fish because it could be considered a "red herring."

paperback novels. I would go through his Zane Grey novels and tear out the extra blank pages at the beginning of the book. I would use them for drawing or sometimes to keep score for a game of cards. Unlined paper was at a premium; we just never had any. There was no stack of bond paper to draw upon, no thick creamy-papered sketchbooks—just our lined Hilroy notebooks for school.

I would also pore through my older sisters' discarded textbooks and see that they, too, drew in the margins or on the extra pages. Mostly they drew women's faces and dresses. I was a lot younger than my sisters, so I would look at these little sketches in their high-school texts and try to draw like that. My older sisters were probably the first artistic influences I had.

That was the extent of art I saw in rural Newfoundland. I never in the world imagined that I would ever be an artist. In fact it seemed utterly impossible.

Then again: it's not like I was pining to become an artist. Even as a young woman, I never considered art school. The thought just never occurred to me. I imagined a job of some kind, of course, but that was all I ever wanted: a job that would allow me to look after myself. I dreamed of owning a house, having a car, and being a professional of some sort. I was always worried about being able to pay the bills, even as a young child. I watched my mother struggle at times to make ends meet and never wanted that. I wanted extra money at the end of my paycheque and I wanted security. It never occurred to me that you could be an artist and have that.

It was a long time after I started hooking rugs that I even considered myself "an artist."

"Scrolls" (30 x 18, 1990). This was the first rug I ever made. Marion Kennedy from Tatamagouche, Nova Scotia, gave me a kit and simply said, "Now hook it" after teaching me one simple stitch.

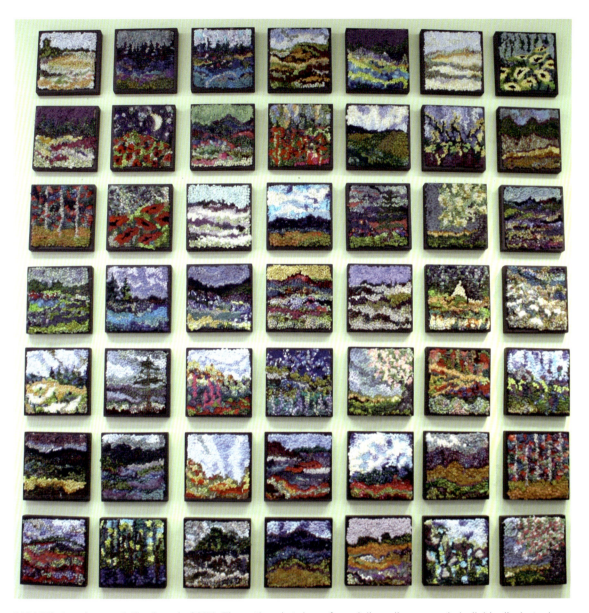

"49 Little Landscapes" (8 x 8 each, 2015). These tiny sketches of my daily walks are made individually, but when I put them together they take on a whole new feeling. I love these tiny rugs that make up a whole; I feel as if I will always hook them.

"Create Beauty Everyday" (19 x 22, 2010). This phrase became the mantra for my studio when Susan Black, another artist, told me, "I think you are doing more than hooking rugs."

Sometimes I would roll that word around in my head, and honestly I just thought it sounded pretentious. Somewhere along the way I came to the idea that it was more important to *act* like an artist than it was to actually *be* one. I just figured if I started acting like an artist—that is: making stuff, going to galleries, reading about art, all the things I imagined artists do—that it might be more useful than wondering whether I was one or not.

I remember visiting John Neville, a really good artist whom I have a lot of respect for. He lived in Halls Harbour, Nova Scotia, for years and operated a studio with his wife, Joyce. One afternoon I was in their studio looking at John's work when he walked in, and it was only through the conversation he was having with his wife that I figured out *he* was the artist. He was so unassuming. There was no beret, I can tell you that. John was plainly dressed, and looked like he might work part-time in a hardware store. That visit, along with many others to working artists throughout Nova Scotia, helped clarify for me that most artists are head-down, hardworking people. Most are not the stereotypical divas we have been taught to believe they are. They are worker bees, compelled to make stuff.

I figured I could be that. I loved to make rugs. The biggest thing about being an artist is making, whether it's hooking rugs, painting, or writing songs. You gotta do the work. So I got to be an artist by acting like one, and by making my rugs. I just did the things I imagined artists doing. I read about them. I studied the work of artists I admired. I went to galleries. I bought art. I immersed myself in a world of art. But most importantly, I tried to make rugs that were unmistakably art. Once I decided I was one, I worked every day at being an artist.

I can hardly believe I have done this for more than twenty-five years. At my best guess, I have made a couple thousand rugs. I have had the grace of a life of making something beautiful. It was never what I set out to do, but once I started hooking rugs it just happened. I could not stop it.

I went to the frame every day with that hook in my hand and pulled loop after loop until I became an artist. As magical as it seems to look back upon it, it really was more of a practical transformation. There was no magic dust sprinkled on me, unless you count being blessed with desire and the willingness to do it.

I simply made rugs, and eventually those rugs became art, and because of that I am an artist.

BEAUTY EVERYWHERE

The first time I came to Cumberland County I was twelve years old, going into grade seven. We rode over on the *Ambrose Shea* ferry. I remember helping my mother pack a lunch for the eighteen-hour ride but being too seasick on the *Shea* to enjoy the Ritz crackers and egg salad sandwiches on my mother's homemade bread.

We drove from Sydney to Amherst and I got lost in the lush green fields. It was the first time I had left Newfoundland, that hard and strong terrace of rock where I belonged. This was something different, this soft plush earth that could grow corn and cucumbers and beans.

It was like the land itself was blessed. Very few people at home—with the exception of Leo Smith who lived up the hill from us—could grow anything except turnip and cabbage.

These two landscapes of my childhood are so different, yet each have a terrific beauty. I love them both, and I want others to love them too—to see them as I see them.

I love it here in Cumberland County, this unspoiled, undeveloped, unrecognized triangle of land barely hanging on to the rest of Canada by the Chignecto Isthmus. It's divided from the rest of Nova Scotia by a toll highway called the Cobequid Pass; the only toll in Nova Scotia. Why are we so special, you might ask, that we charge to get here? We are rural. Beautifully so.

"Green Mountains" (30 x 18, 2018). Sometimes I just need to hook these "field rugs" as I refer to them. It soothes me. Most of them come from scenes I pass while walking or driving.

Things slow down once you cross the Pass. A sparseness comes upon you that makes you sensitive to the landscape around you. There are fewer houses, more trees…and then of course there are those crimson blueberry fields that compel you to pay attention. This county is a work of art.

I say all the time how beautiful it is here. It's like I am trying to convince people. Like I want to own their eyes so they can see it the way I see it. I sometimes wonder why. Why do I care? Why do I want others to believe what I believe, to see what I see?

Well, I suppose it might be because I am an artist in the first place. That is what we are like. We are bound and determined to show what the world is like through our eyes, through our words, through our song. We have this infinite desire to show others how we see it. I don't understand it, that desire. It is just something that wells up inside of me and starts pouring out. Gushing even. Sometimes.

Is it just ego? Well, maybe. I have enough of that. I am always a little disappointed when I am introduced to someone and they do not recognize my name. I am a little embarrassed to

"Advocate Harbour" (46 x 28, 1998). This was based on an antique photo I purchased from Conrad Byers in Parrsboro. Whenever I work from photos I change perspectives and add whatever I want to create a kind of dreamscape. As a result, these rugs never truly depict real places.

tell you that. That is definitely my ego. (Artists are famous for it, after all.) But I have to believe that this desire is more than just ego. Surely it is about more than myself. Surely the spirit enters at this stage and says, "Share what you see, dear, 'cause it's lovely." Surely it is more than ego.

I just feel like in my heart I contain all this beauty and I have to let it out. I have this uncontrollable desire to share the way I see it. Call it passion. Call it wonder. Call it whatever you like. If I did not have it I could never be an artist. See, something happens to me when I am out looking at the world.

Like today, I was out on the Bay of Fundy and I looked at the West Bay Cliff Formation off of Parrsboro and it turned into a hooked rug before my eyes. That is magic. The stone turned into strands of mauve, taupe, and brown wool cloth, all dyed to perfection. The scrubby old pine and spruce hanging on to its top turned into fleece. Honest to Jesus, it did. Imagine! Me just sitting there on a zodiac and parts of the world are turning into this woolen fairyland right before my eyes. The stone is just a bunch of hit-and-miss brown wool lined up to meet the fifty-foot tide below.

"Cliffs" (36 x 24, 2008). Inspired by a boat ride in Placentia Bay, Newfoundland.

"Foxes of Change" (54 x 42, 2019). This rug is about how things are never quite the way you remember them. I know that the Newfoundland of my girlhood is very different from the Newfoundland that exists now.

See, when the world changes itself in front of you it begs you to speak about it. It is too strong to hold in. You are compelled to turn that magic into something tangible. You need to let it out. Big old tears well up in your eyes and sometimes you gasp out loud because inspiration has struck again. And that inspiration, well, she's a tricky thing. She comes and goes whenever she likes, like she owns the place. You cannot hold on to it unless you jot it down, or draw it on a scrap of paper—and even then, it is just a whisper of what you felt in the moment.

And there you are: on the boat, glad the engine is loud and you have your sunglasses on so the people you're with don't think there's something wrong with you as a tear slides down your cheek.

"It's a Mauve Day" (12 x 24, 2014). When I work with greys, I often lean towards mauves as well and soft greens. Grey days are some of my favourites. I find them calming.

MAKING, SIMPLY MAKING

Before I was an artist, I imagined what it might be like. I imagined a person happily sequestered, writing or painting all day. I thought of them attending gallery openings and book launches. I really saw them as someone special. I never imagined that launches and parties only took up a few hours each year. I never thought of the mundane. In my mind, artists lived as they are portrayed on television: a special class of people with berets and cigarette holders. I think it is common to have romantic notions about the creative life. Most people believe it is something separate; there is an allure of mystery to it.

Once and for all, I would like to clear up the allure and solve the mystery: the life of an artist includes getting groceries. It includes cleaning up the messes they are constantly making. It is a life of repetition, of doing the same things over and over again. I think you have to have a special appreciation of the mundane in order to be an artist. You have to really value the simple repetitive tasks that are involved in making what you like to make. It is about creating

"Abstract Mountains" (20 x 32, 2018). Inspired by an image of a mountain range in Labrador. I often layer my landscapes, showing what I imagine to be underneath the earth's surface as part of the image.

"Mystery in the Sky" (24 x 24, 2016). My rugs can be inspired by all kinds of things—a poem, a picture, a novel, or music. This rug, I would have to say, was inspired by the Iris DeMent song "Let the Mystery Be."

"Hot Pink Moose" (24 x 24, 2015). Moose have become elemental in my rugs. They are a symbol of family, strength, and home. The colour choice was just to make it playful; I love the way the hot pink contrasts against the more realistic colours of the barrens.

things that once did not exist, whether that is a hooked rug, a song, a story, a dance, a painting, or numerous other things. Being an artist is about making things.

Most successful artists I know are good at making things. They use their imagination. They are curious. They are inspired. But mostly they make stuff. They work. They show up at the computer, the rug frame, the easel, the guitar, and they sit and try their best. Because they do that most days, every once in a while sparks fly. When these sparks fire, two ideas are tied together and something new appears. The artist gets this idea in their head and they run with it as fast as they can, as far as they can. That is, of course, if they have time. Making things takes lots of time.

Either way, the big idea only showed up because they did.

When you are an artist you carry your ideas around with you all the time. Sometimes they are just old ideas waiting to meet something new. Sometimes they are two ideas that have just met and are still getting to know each other. Ideas are your currency. You know how important they are. You record them; you save them; you value them.

Personally, I go around all the time searching for new ideas and hoping the old ones in my head meet something new. And they do. Sometimes when I least expect it. I know one thing: creative ideas rarely collide when I am looking over my studio financial statements. They require space, and ambiance. They happen when I am out walking alone, or riding my bike, or making a pie. They happen when I see something new or hear a song I've never heard before. They happen when I close my eyes and listen to the sound of a single fiddle, or go for a walk along the shore. They could happen almost

anywhere but they don't much happen at the grocery store, or when I am doing the wash, or meeting with the accountant. But I have to show up for those things, too.

You see, being an artist is a blessed thing but it doesn't make you an exception. It doesn't make you an angel. It is not like in the movies where you walk in the room with a *swoosh* and someone brings you a cocktail. You have to show up day after day, not just to paint or hook or write, but for all the mundane things in between too. All those routine tasks allow you to know the value of the moment, and the beauty of the time you have to make. I always feel that doing all those little things makes me appreciate the time I have to hook.

Being an artist has given me a simple definition for artists: artists make stuff inspired by their own ideas. There is no great mystery. They are the makers, the idea people, and they show up day after day to turn their ideas into reality.

"Shells and Swans" (37 x 56, 2016). The subtle shades in this rug evoked both seashells and swans for me. When I hook abstractly I do not always start out with an idea, just form, and the feeling of the rug creates its title.

SHOWING UP

Sometimes I come to the frame feeling a bit pathetic. It is as if I have nothing new to offer it. I have no idea what to hook. In fact I feel like I have already hooked everything I could imagine. This can go on for a while, maybe through several rugs. It can last for weeks. It does not have anything much to do with how I feel as a whole, it's more about my ideas for my art. At these times I wonder if something new will ever come. I make simple things, but I still make. I hook studio patterns that I made long ago or create big old floor rugs. I hook hit-and-miss designs until something strikes me. The important thing is that I hook. Whatever I make does not matter; I just need to hook. I put my feelings aside and make a mat.

A long time ago an artist told me you just have to show up. You have to show up every day and do the work. It does not matter how you feel. It does not matter if you are inspired. If you show up, inspiration will too…eventually.

"Waves Rise Up To Meet You" (22 x 36 each, 2008). This rug is the story of a marriage; of being together but separate.

"A Life by Land and Sea" (60 inches, 1998). This rug is about the deep traditions of our Atlantic coast: net needles, Celtic crosses, and sailing ships.

After twenty-five years I have learned that the uninspired feeling goes away. Just as in life, you do not have the same zest day after day. Most of us feel a certain level of malaise at times. We find ourselves yearning for something, but we don't know what. We feel there is a hole, an absence of some sort. It is not necessarily depression, just the human condition. I use "we" because it would be too difficult to believe I was alone in this feeling. I know I am not. There are a lucky few of you who have no idea what I mean, but I think there are enough of you who do. We of the human condition sometimes want something, but have no idea what. We feel a sadness for some unexplained reason. We struggle through.

When I feel that sense of melancholic longing come over me, I just try to remember that it will pass. Because it does. It goes away most of the time without me ever knowing how it came or why it lifted. Feelings, even the most intense, do not hold the same intensity forever. When I am sad I try to remember that I won't always be sad. When I am happy I try to savour it, knowing that it too is just temporary. That uninspired feeling, it will go away. I carry this back into my work. *I won't always be showing up at the frame without an idea*, I remind myself. Ideas will come.

I don't use the term "creative block" because I don't think that is what it is. It is just the nature of creative flow. Even the best artists

"Crest of the Wave #2" (13 x 6, 2014). Is there anyone not captivated by waves? I have been since I was a child. They are one of the most interesting and dynamic forms to hook.

"Blue Posies" (40 x 8, 2005). When I look at flowers I am always amazed at their shape; when I hook flowers I like to do it Impressionist-style.

struggle for ideas. I remember famous painter Alex Colville being interviewed on a television show and saying that he would paint more if he had more good ideas. We all have to evaluate the ideas that come to us. No one is standing in a constant steady stream of ideas. Even if they are, they need to assess their ideas and decide which are worth following through on. I try not to worry; I work and wait, and leave some room for ideas to come when they're ready. Sometimes, if I don't have a good idea I just step away from the frame for a few days. They will come when they come. It's a bit like waiting for your grown children to visit; you might not know *when* they are arriving, but they will come. Especially if you prepare things nicely for them. So you might as well just keep busy until they arrive.

The part about preparing the place for your children is important, though. They come to expect it. In my experience inspiration is no different. She wants you to keep busy and not bother her with a bunch of "just checking in" texts, but she also wants you to be happy and to enjoy yourself. Like your children, she doesn't want to feel guilty thinking about you home, sitting sadly waiting for her. She wants you to be like Emerson, and "live in the sunshine, swim in the sea, and drink the wild air." She expects you to show up regularly, but also to get out of the studio and see and breathe and feel because she needs that too.

So that is what I do. I take time off. I keep busy with smaller projects, but I also take time to retreat. A good book, a long walk, visits with friends, a day trip, or whatever food your soul needs, feed it.

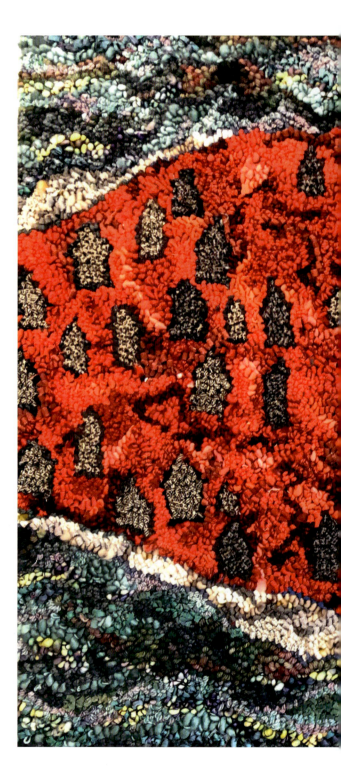

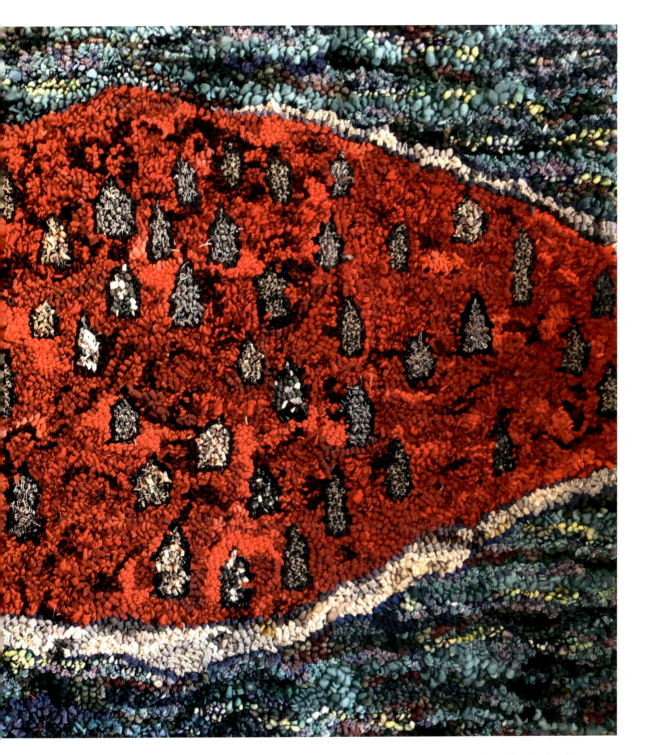

"Red Island" (42 x 32, 2018). There were around sixty families left on Red Island, Newfoundland, when it was resettled in the 1950s, and most of them moved to the community I grew up in. Sometimes I hook these resettled communities as vibrant places full of life, and other times as the lost places they are.

TIDE AND TIME

When I went out the door of my childhood home, I would grab a dried capelin off Mr. Bernie's flake. It was kind of like fish jerky: slight and salty and silver with a thin flaky tail. There is nothing like that childhood freedom of swiping a capelin off a flake on the way to nowhere. So many times as a child I left the house with no destination in mind. I just went out and met up with whomever there was to meet up with, and did whatever there was to do. It was a loose kind of feeling.

When I would walk out the door I could feel the ocean in the air. Grey mornings lined with a veil of fog; sometimes I could not see the beach, but I could smell the salt and hear the boats turning back toward the wharf. There was a bay below our house and I always felt as if I were walking toward it, no matter the direction I was actually headed. Not only was it an enormous part of our landscape, it was also on my mind all the time. I was always on the beach collecting rocks or climbing hills. It was my place. It remains my place, but in memory.

I think of the view from my childhood home nearly every day. Those hard rounded

"A Fish Story" (40 x 40, 1996). When I was a child, the fish were so big that the head and tail would spill over the sink. This is a self portrait, and honest: it's not a fish story.

rocks were in softer shades—I can still picture them under my feet—and I would stare down at the grey-blue palette, looking for any contrast that washed ashore. I can feel the ridges of the hard-shelled white barnacles that were so deeply attached to the blackest rocks. I grew up by the sea, and the sea is in me. The water was rough, so I never went in, ever. The closest I got was going to the edge to fill a bucket full of capelin as they were rolling in on the waves. The Placentia coast was cold and ragged and beautiful. It was meant more for livelihood than pleasure, so I stayed on the shore and took note of every colour and texture. Hours I spent there, doing very little.

I don't spend much time in Newfoundland now. I live in Nova Scotia, where the sea is different. I go to Amherst Shore. I go to Advocate. I go to Parrsboro. The sea itself is different but the feeling is the same; the feeling that it is okay to float. Suddenly you understand that tides come and go, and although the water never stops moving it never goes far. There it is right before you, always moving yet going nowhere.

It slows you down.

Then you are reminded.

Of what you are like.

Of what life is like.

Of Ecclesiastes, that old man in the Bible, who knew that everything that is done was done before. And that's okay.

There is a quote I love so much from Isak Dinesen: "The cure for anything is salt water; sweat, tears, or the sea." The ocean is like a tonic; there is a certain truth to that. It turns

"Visiting on the Way From Church" (14 x 24 each, 1996). Growing up, our life centred around church and school. My mother and her friends traditionally wore bandanas and walked down over the hill together to church.

something in us, and helps us understand that it is okay to tread water. It is okay if things don't happen as quickly as you'd like. It might even be okay even if they don't happen at all. And you don't need mindfulness training or yoga or tapes or podcasts—you are just being you. You are you because the water is floating by and you are on the shore watching it and you are not too worried about anything. And while you are watching it you know all this is true.

And then you walk away from the water and everything starts up again: the tonic wears off; you speed up; life resumes. The world is back and you are as big a part of it as you ever were. But you are altered because you know that behind those spruce trees, there remains the sea and you can always go back.

I don't know exactly what it is about this cure, the sea, that makes it so, but I do know it to be true. There is a depth in our relationship with it, a sense of belonging in those who grow up by it. We are called to it, and if we don't answer that call it we are at a loss.

I still rely on the ocean to bring me home. It might be a different body of water in a different place from where I grew up, but it achieves the same end. It calls on me to be present, to rest, and to enjoy my life. When I seek inspiration I go to it, not just physically but also in my memory. Both are wells of ideas and dreams that have sustained me (and my work) for over twenty-five years. I am so thankful I grew up by the sea and still remain close to it.

"Funky Fish" (12 x 24, 1999). This is one of my favourite kits we have made in the studio over the years.

"Seacoast 3"
(17 x 36, 2018).
A combination of
water bubbles,
seaweed, fish scales;
together they lay on a
deep blue sea.

STYLE IS THE THING
YOU CALL YOUR OWN

I have never been great at drawing. I draw roughly and quickly and quite badly most of the time. I do not put pen to paper and immediately see things appear before me. I work at it. I learn, I practice, I imitate, and then I change it. Over time those changes have come to define my art. If I were to describe "my style" to you, it would be the soft shoulders of my people, the scratchy brush and scrub in my fields, the slanted roofs of my houses. These lines define my drawing, and over time I have come to appreciate it for what it is.

I knew I did not have a natural talent for drawing detail from the time I was about seven. I would watch my cousin draw; he would meticulously spend hours on the same piece of paper while I would go through sheet after sheet. At the age of seven I never saw this as "different styles," instead I saw it as good and bad. There is no such thing really when it comes to the way you choose to draw. You draw the way your eye sees, the way your mind sees.

When I was little I just thought my cousin could draw better than me and that was that. Now I know that we draw *differently*—he can still draw more realistically, is more precise, and takes the time to render things exactly as he

"The Sound of a Single Fiddle" (38 x 62, 2002). Is there any better sound than a single fiddle? This was one of the first times I tried making the roofs of my houses a little tilted.

"The Seven Sisters" (48 x 70, 1999). I am one of seven sisters, and often use multiples of seven when designing rugs and patterns. My sisters are all good, kind, strong women and I have always been proud to be one of them.

sees them. It is a gift that he has and I appreciate it. I have come to understand, though, that my way of drawing is my own and that I have a different gift. Understanding and appreciating your own gifts was not a concept I grew up with in the 1970s, when homogeneity was more important than diversity. It is something I came to in adulthood, this understanding that being different could be a good thing.

Over the years I have learned that with patience and practice I can render things realistically, but it does not necessarily make me happy to do it. I don't love the process of sitting there, sketching little lines and trying to get something to look just so. Just as I don't enjoy hooking fine strips of wool and making a rug out of three- and four-cut. I can do it; I just don't enjoy it. When you don't enjoy something it is still possible to become "good" at it, but it is hard work because there is so little pleasure in it.

I have chosen instead to do what I love, and to do it as often as I can. I like big, soft, loose lines. I like drawings that lead me to see something other than what is on the paper (or in my case the burlap or linen). I like creating a sense of something new, of looking at an object or landscape and bringing it down to the few essential lines. Those simple line drawings of nudes sketched with five or six loose lines by famous artists, well, they make me swoon. They make me wish I were in the image. They transport me because they are what I love and understand and appreciate. They make me want to be a better artist. They make me aspire to be more than I am right now.

When I was a little girl I did not know there were different kinds of good drawing, so I stopped drawing altogether. I did not know yet what I loved. Knowing what you love comes with maturity for most of us, although some of us know from the time we are little. My cousin knew when he was little that he loved to do things perfectly. He eventually became a plastic surgeon and he is good at it. He remains a meticulous drawer and painter, and he does both even more beautifully now than he did when we were young.

There are so many kinds of beautiful, so many ways to be right, and so many kinds of good. Thus, as artists, there are so many kinds of style, and if you just focus on what you do and pour your hear into it, style will emanate.

Over the course of a twenty-five-year career, I have come to appreciate that although I am not precise, there are things about that I can embrace. After all, finding out what you are good at and making the very best of it is your job in life. I am lucky that somewhere along the way I learned there are hundreds of different ways of drawing, and that I am good at one of them.

I have learned to value what I am good at, to see it for what it is, and not feel diminished by the talents of others. It has taken too long, probably, but it has happened. I am still moved by the style of realists but I don't define my own talents by theirs anymore. I am another kind of artist. Perhaps it is simpler, more naive, perhaps it is worse, or perhaps it is better. I really can't say, because meaning is derived from those who consume art, not necessarily those who create it; every person who looks at art defines that "meaning" for themselves.

The job of the artist is to love what you do as you make art. That does not mean there is no struggle—there is bound to be some!—but the struggle is not always fuelled by anguish. Sometimes it is borne of fatigue, boredom, or a physical challenge. Each struggle is personal. Regardless, you should still enjoy the act of making. If someone teaches you in a certain way, you might find you need to adapt that teaching to better suit your style, and that's okay! Be sure to find your own way.

Because if you want to be an artist, your way is the only way.

"Flowers" (20 x 20 each, 2008). I think it is so important to remember that beauty is enough when you are making rugs—or any kind of art, really. That is why sometimes I just hook flowers. Making something beautiful is enough in itself; there doesn't always have to be layers of meaning.

"Salt Water and Southeast Winds" (24 x 46, 2005). My early field rugs used lots of fleece from Delia Burge's sheep, which I still use today. I love to write in my rugs, even though it can be a bit difficult to read. Often, the words are more about the process and an element of design than meaning.

RIDE THE WAVES

I live on an isthmus and am almost completely surrounded by water except for the Tantramar Marshes that connect us to New Brunswick. This proximity, combined with my childhood by the sea, means water holds a certain prominence in my rugs.

But I also remember watching the water one day as a helicopter flew over the Northumberland Strait searching for three fishermen lost at sea. I saw ominous foreboding in it that day. I saw how the same tidal flats my children built castles and moats on could fill up angrily, leaving anguish in the wake. As a child I remember a whole family going down in a boat as it crossed Placentia Bay. It scared me so; this story floated around in my mind, making me anxious and fearful of the ocean's power.

I am afraid of the water. It can swallow you whole and never notice. It can turn on you in an instant. It rises up like an angry beast just because the sun hid her head and the wind came up. As lovely as it is to sit and watch the sea, there is no reason to trust her. So as beautiful as the sea might be when I hook it, I am also sometimes hooking its force, its raw power, and its destructiveness. Those things are so at odds with the tranquil deep-blue sea of a sunny day, of walking dogs on tidal flats, and of sun hats and bathing suits, but they, too, are embedded in the sea stories of my mats as I hook them.

But still, I swim. I put my head under the water. I ride in boats. I love it all, but I know who is the maiden, and I know that it is the sea that decides the fate of the maiden. As cautious as I am in the water, I still love it. When the tide is right, I like to swim in the sea before I go to work in the morning, and then dip in again just as the moon is coming up. It is this kind of living with the sea that lets me hook the sea. I try to also bring the calm feeling that comes

"The Swimmers" (20 x 34, 2006). This rug is about being comfortable in your own skin and how that comes with age. I never had that as a young woman, but I did gain some of it in my forties and I am so thankful for it.

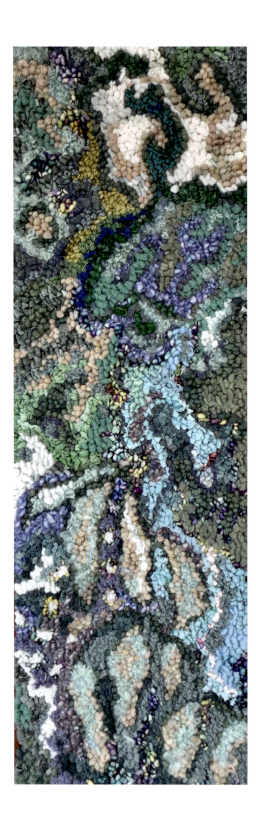

from those swims and those walks along the shore to my mats. This duality is endlessly fascinating to me.

I love hooking water scenes because in my rugs I am in control. I get to tame the water, and control the force at which she flows. I decide the weather of the day. I know that I can contend with the gale-force winds, and I know how high the tide will rise. I know who can sail it, and that they'll safely come into port. In my rugs I have a knowledge and freedom that is unbeknownst to the fragile human.

How powerful is that? Well, it feels pretty good. As a creator, you get to decide the beginning, middle, and end of any story you tell. All this power you hold over something you make. It is one of the only times in life you are really, truly, completely in control. I have control over my mats in a way that I will never have in life.

It's a fascinating paradox: in art, you are in complete control as long as you let go. Well, what the hell does that mean? For me it means I can make major decisions—sort of steer the ship—but if I want things to really work out, I need to let go so the flow can happen, and creativity can take its course. Every time I try to exercise full control when I hook rugs—when I ignore a creative wave and stubbornly stick to my original thought—it imposes a kind of rigidity onto what I am making that I can see in the finished rug. And it isn't good. It's like if I try too hard to get it "right," there is a stiffness to it.

Making things, just a simple act of hooking a rug, is powerful because it lets you live another life—an interior life. You start to recognize metaphors for your own life in the process of creating, and you are grateful to have the chance to steer the course for a change. Sometimes, you'll find the artistic decisions you make along

"Seacoast 1" (right, 21 x 34, 2018) and "Seacoast 2" (left, 10 x 33, 2018).
I remember leaning over the railing of the ferry that ran from Newfoundland to Nova Scotia and seeing that the water was green. When I mentioned that to my father, he replied, "Yes, honey, the water is blue-green."

"Mermaid and Moonsnails" (12 x 42, 2012). I love her hit-and-miss hair and the decorative fish tail.

the way change you. They give you space. They give you time to lose yourself and time to find yourself. It becomes more than just the thing you are making; it is the making that really matters.

So it's this crazy balance between hanging on and letting go, between steering and letting the wind take you in the right direction. I imagine it is a bit like being on the water in a sailboat (though I have no real knowledge of this, and poor sea legs to boot). But there is probably a parallel, because a good sailor needs to be flexible when handling a boat.

When I hook water, I try to incorporate all of these things. I try not to just think of the "good" or the "bad," but of what I know. And as always—as with everything—there is both. My mats with big waves reflect the ocean's force, but my mats of women at the shore are more about reflecting on those fine days when passing time feels endless.

It is because of this duality that I will never stop wanting to hook the sea. It is so much more than just blue. So much more than a picture-perfect sunrise or sunset. It is a study in love, in loss, in endurance. As I hook, I think of my grandfather in a dory being shaken to his core and tossed like a toy as he tried desperately to row home. I think of the intrepid Irish people who set sail for a new home so long ago and settled the rock-hard coast of southern Newfoundland, paving a way for me to write, to hook, to be anything I want. I imagine all that history when I hook the ocean. I carry in my DNA all the sea stories that came before me, of my father building dories, and my grandmother hooking rugs of the neighbours' boats.

It is so much more than blue.

"Seaweed and Starfish" (26 x 51, 2014). I really like hooking what I imagine to be floating under the sea or in a tidal pool. I love the freedom to let the wool flow easily from one shade to another.

"Into the Sky" (24 x 24, 2016). This rug was part of a collection called "The Very Mention of Home" that is now owned by the Art Gallery of Nova Scotia.

RUG FRAME

This week we started putting a big antique rug-hooking frame on the sidewalk outside the studio. It is made of dark aged wood with handmade wooden gears at the end. You know it is special as soon as you look at it. You will never see another one quite like it.

After I had been hooking for about ten years, the woman who taught me to hook, Marion Kennedy, brought it to me as a gift. This surprised me, since I never knew Marion very well.

I was always grateful to her for teaching me the way she did: she prepared a kit for me and told me to complete it after showing me how to hook one simple stitch. When she mentioned that my stitches weren't even, I went to pull them out but she held back my hand and said, "No, you'll get better as you go along. Finish it." I have been using the Marion Kennedy Method of Teaching ever since—and I am grateful to her.

I only ever met Marion a couple of times. The first time, she taught me how to hook; the second time, she came to gift me the frame; and the third time, I visited her in a seniors' home when she no longer seemed to be aware of what was going on around her. A few years later I attended her memorial service at Pictou Lodge. It was there that I learned most about her from her friends and family who were gathered to speak about her life and all she had accomplished.

It amazes me, though, what an impact she had on my life for someone I met only three times. When she taught me how to hook, she likely had no idea she was part of charting the course of my life. I sometimes wonder whether if she had been a different kind of teacher I would I be hooking at all…if she had been fussy and directive with me, whether I might never have continued. Instead she was tolerant and supportive, but kind of bossy still. She did not care how I hooked, she just wanted me to hook. She knew that once I finished my first piece I

"Lighthouse" (34 x 18, 1993). In the beginning, my work was more simplistic and direct. It was folk art, I suppose, but that changed over time in a very honest way as I became more aware of art and was influenced by it.

would know that I could do it, and from there I could figure out just how I wanted to hook.

So that old frame is exactly where it should be: out where anyone walking down the street can have a go at it and try to hook. For years I kept it stored away, justifying it as a piece of furniture that needed to be safeguarded and properly stored. Then last week I decided if that frame was really going to do its job and inspire people to hook, it needed to be outside. Why save these things as icons? They might as well be used. Marion gave me that frame because she felt I would look after it. She entrusted it to me so that it would have a life.

On Saturday as I crossed the street from my studio to 30 Church, which I do ten times a day, a boy of about fourteen was looking at the frame with his older sister. I stopped to see if they were interested in learning, and I showed him how to hook. When I came back about twenty minutes later, he was still hooking and his sister was inside the studio looking around. Now that boy and his sister will always know how to hook a rug, and maybe one day he will make one, or maybe he will show someone else how to make one.

Either way, the frame is definitely where it belongs.

"Irish Angels Watching over Bay Girls" (18 x 54, 1999). Thankfully, I always carry with me the comfort that someone is watching over me. Given my name is Fitzpatrick, they might well be Irish.

WALK AWAY

Sometimes when I hook I can feel a jumpiness in me. That's a sign: I am unsettled, and it is manifesting physically. On the nights I stayed up too late or lost sleep worrying over something, I arrive at the frame with only my body present. I hook, but it just ends up being loops on a backing. The *feeling* is absent. At those times I get up and go for coffee. I leave the studio altogether and walk. I sometimes drive to Sackville, the next town over, and walk into Blooms, the local flower shop. I let someone else's inspiration renew me. I sometimes pick up a book—a good mystery—and get carried away with someone else's story. I never force myself to hook unless I feel like it, because it is the *feeling* that matters, not the hooking itself.

"Renewal" is such an important word if you want to create beauty every day; and you cannot create beauty without immersing yourself in it.

If I find myself struggling to come up with the right colour combination or pattern, the only answer is to walk away. An afternoon nap, a brisk walk, a cup of tea. Any distraction will do. I don't pore over my work or face it as a struggle; I just need to get away from the frame. The only answer for me is to forget about what I am doing and focus on something else entirely. I cannot force the right colour to appear in the rug. Sometimes I just have to wait.

As I walk away, I throw my last colour choice down on the frame knowing I will come back fresher, or at least with new possibilities. Sometimes I think about the colours while I am away from the rug, especially if it is overnight. I close my eyes and imagine the possibilities. Usually, though, I just get lost in some new activity.

I very rarely pull out large parts of anything I have hooked. Years ago an older woman—a very traditional rug hooker—visited my studio. She said, "I am not part of that hook-it-and-pull-it-out crowd" in reference to herself. It resonated with me. She said it as if there were two kinds of rug hookers: those who hook it and pull it out, and those who don't. Well, there are always more than two kinds of anything, but it seems to me that some people like to unhook their rugs as much as they like hooking them. I have seen people hook in and pull out colours in the same area of the rug over and over again and get no further ahead. Sometimes the rug

My hooking chair and frame.

"Moon Over the Mountains" (20 x 36, 2012).

hooker just needs to step back or even just focus on another area of the rug. That compulsion to get it "just right" can be disabling.

If I have a niggling feeling that an area needs to be taken out, I wait until after I have hooked the whole rug. If something is still not a fit at the end, then it is fair to take it out. The thing is, in the middle of the process I cannot always tell what is good and what is not. Every time I add a new colour, every colour that is already in the rug changes. This is what colour does: one colour relates to and affects another. This is why I often cannot tell if a colour is "good" in the rug when I am in the middle of making it, because that colour will shift and evolve as I add new ones.

I usually assess a colour before I hook it in: I lay one colour down on the frame and look at it, then take it away and lay another down. If I need to, I hook a few stitches and then make the decision to carry on or not. Sometimes you just have to see those few stitches in the context of the mat to know what you are seeing. I try to go by feeling and what looks good, but I am cautious and deliberate. I try to pick colours carefully but with an open mind. Unfortunately this often leads to me just staring blankly at a bunch of wool. Sometimes I walk around the studio with a swatch in one hand and look dreamily at what is around. Even here in this big studio full of wool I sometimes cannot find the right colour.

I like to say that if a colour seems slightly wrong or out of place, then it might be just right. You want to go for the odd matches, the irregular, the unexpected; that is where the beautiful surprises emerge. I love how teal and gold sing each other's praises in a mat. Colours can bring out the best in each other, like bright red and lime, with just a touch of black on white. It is also how you can develop better colour work

in your rugs. You need to push yourself into new combinations so your work can grow and change. I am often tempted to reuse colour combinations that I like, but I try to push myself out of that comfort zone. And I do have to push, because those old combinations really work. It is so easy, so comforting, but my soul just screams no. That little art soul says, "Use me right, Deanne; strengthen me." So I concede and I try to add a new shade, find a new way, and set off a new round of comfortable choices that I love.

The other thing worth noting is that your interest in colours may change over time. It could follow trends and fashion, but it could also just evolve based on what you're interested in. There were years when I was not at all interested in hot pink, and years where I could not stop using it. My love of colours subsides and flourishes depending on my heart, I suppose. What I consider beautiful at one time may no longer be beautiful to me at another time, and that is a lovely thing.

As for actually making a rug, when I pick a colour I know I am making a conscious choice. I don't just arbitrarily throw a bunch of colours on the frame and go at it. It looks like that when I watch myself hook. It just seems like I am pulling colours out of nowhere. The truth is most of my colour choices are really deliberate and thought out. Choosing colours is probably the most important decision I make once the rug design is laid out. Hooking this way means I pull out less, and hook more. Every time I add a colour I change the rug.

For me, colour and texture are why I still hook. Of course I also enjoy the physical motion of hooking, but it is the creative experimenting that excites me, and makes me curious, and pushes me further. I love the potential in rug-hooking, and because there are so many

The Great Wall of Colour. I take a lot of love and pride in making my studio beautiful. We get visitors from all over the world and I like them to feel that they have really arrived in a beautiful place.

"Women in Paisley" (38 x 18, 2007). There are eight women in this rug even though I often depict sevens. One of my seven sisters' friends bought this rug because she is like part of our family.

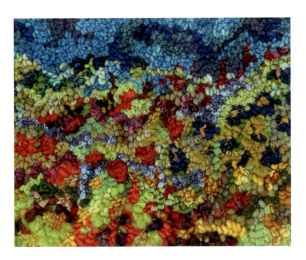

"Undergrowth Garden" (10 x 14, 2012).

colours and textures to combine, I know there is no way I can ever reach a limit. The possibilities shift and change over time as I find a new shade, or a new yarn.

I always tell new people who are just starting that there is only one stitch to learn but it is what you can do with colour and design that really counts.

ON THE BICYCLE AGAIN

I was about twelve, I was riding my bicycle down the big hill I grew up on and suddenly got scared. A wave of fear overtook me and I panicked. I forgot how to use the brakes. My bike went careening through the intersection and I tumbled over a concrete wall.

That was the first time I had an accident on a bike. I got up and rode my bike back home.

The second time was a similar story. I was riding down that same hill, had a wave of excited panic, and flipped over a guardrail. I got up again and rode my bike, but I became nervous. I was alone each time so at least the humiliation was private and personal.

I chalked these falls up to my not being good at biking, and pretty much stopped riding altogether. I was too young to realize that it was not the act of riding, but the sudden waves of fear that were causing me problems. It took me years to understand that. Those flashes of dread have came over me all my life—at one time or another I have worried about the possibility of just about everything. It took me a long time to get back on the bike; I never rode again until I was forty-seven.

The first day I took my bike out I was riding down a hill and a boy yelled, "Nice bike!" I yelled back that it was the first time I had rode in thirty-five years. The next day I tried the bike again down the same hill, and the same boy was there. He yelled, "You're still at it." When I rode down that hill on the bicycle and heard that boy yell at me I felt like I took something back that I had been missing a very long time.

My friend once said to me that there is nothing worse than being afraid when there is nothing to be afraid of; she ought to know, as she struggled with this all her life. I, too, let it get in the way. I have worried needlessly about small things I ultimately had no control over. I still do sometimes. I fret and think too much and too long and go over scenarios in my head. This worrying is just part of me, and I have to constantly work at not letting it be too powerful a force in my life.

There is one place, though, where I am fearless: when I make my rugs. I never worry about the outcome. I am not afraid to waste my time. I do not care what others think of them. I love it when they like them, of course, but that does not dominate my thoughts as I am making them. I make every one of them for myself. I

"July, August, and September" (14 x 14 each, 2008). The same landscape with different fields of colour. I love hooking spruce trees as a background; in many ways I feel spruce woods have been the backdrop for my life.

"Women in Bandanas" (20 x 34, 2005). I grew up with these women watching over me. They had curlers in their hair in the daytime, and bandanas around their curls in the evening.

never worry how they might turn out bad, or won't sell. I don't care if they are ugly because I trust myself that they will not be. I know the brakes are there when I need them, but mostly I just ride. I hook like there is no possible way the bike is going to crash.

You need that fearlessness in order to grow in your work. You need to design like it does not matter, hook like no one cares. Choose colours like you are Kaffe Fassett, one of the world's most famous fibre artists. I hook like I am free. I hook like I want to get to the finish line; I am deliberate and thoughtful about how I get there, but I am getting there no matter what.

Rug-hooking is a lot like riding a bicycle down a safe country path: all you have to do is ride.

"Fuchsia in the Trees" >
(24 x 24, 2018).
This rug was part of series that explored the lushness of trees, swamps, and greenery. I experimented with shades of green I do not typically use.

HARD NOT TO COMPARE

"Comparison is the thief of happiness." Surely you have read some variation of this quote in your Facebook feed. Perhaps it has appeared in beautiful typography painted on reclaimed something or other, or it was pinned to a Pinterest board you follow. The message is everywhere. Not just this one, but it is the one on my mind today.

There was a time when I loved a good quote. I would come across one and it would make me think. Now I am inundated with them; there are a million little bits of wisdom that we know to be true, and they pop up everywhere. It is so easy to read them, to agree with them. Yet it is so hard to live them, no matter how many times they pop up. Finding them is easy; living them is the challenge.

Still, perhaps we need those gentle reminders on our fridge, above our desk, on our coffee mug. At least I do. I am so perfectly human that I constantly need to be reminded I have work to do. Even though I know something to be true, the actual day-to-day living it out, well, I suck at that.

Myself, I struggle with comparison. Many people I know do. It is not easy to admit because it makes you seem like such an arsehole. Why do you care what the other fella is doing? What he looks like, or how high his grass is? What does it matter? Yet it does. We're always looking at what the other fella is doing. We have eyes to see and minds to think, and it is hard not to notice.

Once I was walking with a friend on the marsh and a woman's name came up.

I said, "There is something about her that bugs me."

My friend said, "What is it?"

I said, "I think it is because she is beautiful and lovely."

We both laughed out loud. Our laughter rang out loud across the marsh grass like the wind. It rolled out of us, one big belly laugh after another, riding that undulating grass, reminding us what we were like.

"Up and Down the Coast" (32 x 14, 2003). This is how the story gets around. You say, "I only told my sister," and before you know it, it's all over town.

"Don't Rock the Boat" (24 x 24, 2016). This rug is about the nature of home. Families who live together know not to rock the boat.

My friend knew what I meant. It was the comparison thing. When I saw or thought of that lovely woman (and she is that) I thought less about her and more about myself. She was thinner, more beautiful, accomplished, educated, kind, and sophisticated.

Notice the comparison.

Yet I know that we are all beautifully and fearfully made (Psalms). I know that my own life is full of grace. Still, I ponder the grace of someone else as if her gifts reflect my faults. It is a weakness of confidence perhaps, but I believe it is more than that. I believe it is part of the human condition. We evaluate, judge, think, and feel. We are all of that. And it is so wonderful.

And what makes us wonderful also weakens us. Our strength is our weakness; it is such a shame.

I know I am not alone. Sometimes people ask me how I get so much done. I remind them that between my two businesses, there are ten women who work for me. But I should also remind them that I live in the shadows of my own thoughts, struggling to be good, to be more, to be better. Intellectually I might know I am good enough, but those doubts creep in and challenge me regularly. I should tell them that I, too, wonder how other people do so much, give so much, and are so good. I should let them know that they are not alone in their wonder; that I am wondering the same thing.

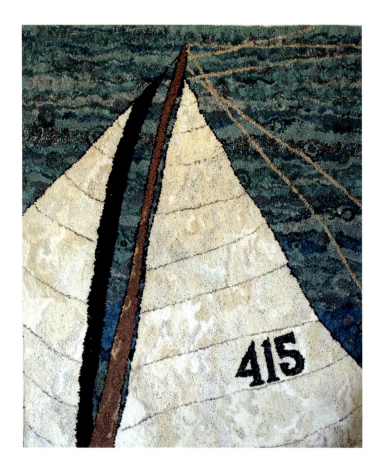

"March Sails" (50 x 58, 2016). I have only been sailing twice in my life, but I find it magnificent. In a generation my family has lost all its knowledge of boats and the water. It was second nature to my father and his family when he was a boy.

QUARTER AND A PENNY

Years ago my friend was attending university and was walking across campus to visit a girl in residence. She was a good friend of his, but something about her always niggled him. It seemed that whatever he did, she made it clear that she had done it better. On the way to her residence he looked down and saw a quarter. He picked it up and put it in is pocket. As soon as he arrived he told her his good news. She smiled and said, "Yesterday I found a quarter and a penny."

Inside he just cringed.

So "a quarter and a penny," my friend will say to me when he senses a little one-upmanship going on. Then we share a laugh.

We all have those friends who feel the need to constantly outdo us. No sooner do they look at your new kitchen countertop than they begin talking about what they should do with their kitchen. Sometimes it is a companionable thing. Other times it feels like they are more interested in themselves and what they are going to do. And what they are going to do is outdo you. They can't help it. They don't even notice they are like that. They might be lovely people, but

"Gone Mod" (24 x 40, 2004). I made this rug one January after a particularly tiring time. I just needed to hook but I had no great ideas so I did something very traditional. I have always felt, though, that this rug looks very modern.

"Fiddleheads" (26 x 26, 2010). I pick fiddleheads sometimes because I love their swirl, and how they grow near streams and brooks in the forest. They are part of the brightness of spring.

they exhaust me. If you've got a quarter, they just have to have a quarter and a penny. Their boat is a little longer, their car a little faster, and their trip a little grander. They don't seem to notice it about themselves but others notice it about them. You might guess that there is always someone who has to be the best, or have the most. The truth is, there is always someone with more. There really is no keeping up. There is always someone richer, someone luckier. Stuff is just stuff; there can always be more added to the pile.

Humans are so fluid and our parameters are always changing. What we want today will be different tomorrow. There is no keeping up with the Joneses because the Joneses turn into the Smiths, who turn into the Browns. The sooner you realize that life should be more about keeping on rather than keeping up, the happier you will be.

Imagine if, instead of becoming richer we all decided to become kinder, or wiser, or better, or smarter. What if we turned our desire for more stuff into something greater?

Personally, I understand the attraction of a ruby to a crow. I get it. I am so easily distracted by the pretty, and so often bored with what I already have. But what if instead of upping the ante we said the pot is already big enough?

Imagine that.

MEET ME

"Meet me at the bridge at noon," read the text. It sounded so romantic. In actuality, though, it was my friend Denise and we were getting together to visit my friend's new bookstore. Sheree Fitch had just opened Mabel Murple's Book Shoppe and Dreamery in River John, and we were going to meet at the bridge to go down together. I have known Denise for a long time. Our children were in elementary school together. There were play dates and sleepovers over the years that linked us together, and through those links we forged a friendship.

There were lots of different connections but it was only when we started knitting together that I really came to know her, and that she really became my friend. I cannot tell you what it is about handwork that brings people together, but it does. There is something that comes with that common desire to make and see things to completion that seems to bless relationships. That inner desire to make is an aggressive force inside of a lot of people. Oddly enough, that aggressive force can lead to a calm passivity.

When I knit or hook or draw, the world goes on around me while I am lost in a kind of wonderment. If someone is doing the same beside me, they understand that feeling of getting lost in the flow of the work. They too

I have been blessed with so many good people over the years helping me in the studio. There is no way I could do this work without them.

"Two Madonnas of Church Street" (30 x 51, 2012). At the top of Church Street one day when I was driving home, Dona Morris and Donna Gibson were singing and carrying their laundry across the road. I stopped to talk to them and they came out to the house that afternoon so I could draw them.

"Moose, Spruce, and Pines" (36 x 36, 2017). For me, moose symbolize strength, home, and my father. Artistically speaking, I love silhouettes and what happens when you outline them. This rug hangs in my kitchen.

understand the joy of made by hand as they look at the rug on the floor, the quilt on the bed, the sweater on their baby. You can't explain it unless you make it.

It is like you both know there is somewhere to go when the pressure is heavy or the worry is a burden; somewhere to hide from the stress of work, a place to settle your mind. You know the comfort that comes from crossing hand over hand for hours at a time. You can do it together or you can do it alone. Either way it strengthens friendship. You talk about your colours, your designs, your plans. You speak of who you plan to give it to, or where you plan to put it. You share an understanding of the handmade.

I watch it in others, too. I see the women at my workshops make fast relationships. To me a "material girl" is one who sees the beauty in making things with fabric or wool. Sorry,

Madonna, I know that is not what you were thinking when you wrote that song. I see these material girls travel across North America with their material friends. It is that woman you share the joy of making things with so much that you'll cross the miles to do it together in a studio someplace you have never heard of. Someplace like Amherst, Nova Scotia.

So that is what it's like: through handwork you learn to count on someone, and they learn that they, too, can count on you. You hit the road together; you share secrets. She is your material girl, the one who understands your obsession with fabric and wool and fibre, and because of that you share each other's stories and you keep them close to your chest.

And if she calls you to meet her at the bridge at noon, you do.

"Blueberry Fields" (40 x 54, 2001). This was one of my first abstract rugs. I remember another artist friend looking at it and I could sense they thought I was going in the wrong direction. This happened often over the years, but I always felt it was important to push myself.

SO MANY GOOD IDEAS

Salted Smoked Split Herring said the little wooden boards that lay in a box in her studio.

"Here, have one," she said.

I took it, not sure if I wanted it or not. I thought I did but was not sure what to do with it. It was an odd little gift.

That was what Gabby was like. She saw things like an artist, and I loved that about her. She kept ephemera like it was gold.

I found Gabby through her brother. I had been in an art show in Moncton at the Aberdeen Cultural Centre with her brother Romeo Savoie. The show was called Art en Direct and featured a small group of contemporary artists all working to create individual pieces over several days.

Romeo said, "My sister Gabby hooks rugs, but not like you."

I was not sure what he meant. I was out of my element: a young anglophone woman, barely an artist yet, with all these well-

"Bella Garden 1 (right) and 2" (20 x 20 each, 2016). Soft shades of mauve and blue with cream is a favourite combination of mine. I often find myself hooking flowers in the dead of winter; a promise of spring.

established Acadian painters. I was naïve enough not to care too much, and curious enough to enjoy it. I left that show wondering about Gabby. Who was this Acadian woman who hooked rugs "not like me." And was that good or bad?

That summer I got Gabrielle Robichaud's phone number from Romeo, and I went to visit her in her cordwood house on the bay in Barachois, New Brunswick.

I discovered that she hooked rugs, painted, collected, and created. She had little bits of everything everywhere, and though I knew I could never be like that, I loved it. Her rugs were indeed not like mine; they were her own. Her rugs were playful and imaginative and sculptural.

I had no desire to hook the way she did, but I loved it. She would hook on chicken wire and sculpt it. She would hook any kind of

"Flower Pot" (8 x 12, 2008). Our kitchen floor was tiled when I was a child in red, white, and black...I think. That's how I remember it, anyway. I love putting the tile element in floors and on tables in my rugs.

material. She would make with no purpose in mind, just make for the sake of making. I loved the way her mind worked. She was full of possibility and she was so quietly happy to share all that possibility with me. When two artists meet and feel compelled to share ideas it is such a lovely thing. It is like you are communicating on another level. You don't really talk about each other, you talk about ideas.

Once at my studio Gabby asked me, "Do you speak French?"

I said, "No, I am sorry. I wish I did."

Gabby shook her head sadly and said, "I wish you did, too, you are missing out on so many good ideas."

I knew what she meant. I love the French and the Acadian way with art, and I definitely do feel that things are lost in translation and I am missing out. Sometimes there is just no accurate way of sharing without a common language. To talk about ideas, you really do need language. We shared an art spirit, and that was lovely, but I still feel I missed a lot.

What I did learn from Gabby is that so much possibility exists in your own mind. It can limit you—and it does sometimes—but it can also free you. As artists we often live in sheltered small worlds surrounded by our own ideas, or similar ideas. We cultivate a space for ourselves, not just in our studios but also in our minds where we work out those ideas.

Gabby and I visited back and forth a few times and even though we had different styles, we really enjoyed each other's company. It was always an artist-to-artist visit. Every time I was with her I came home feeling wiser and more inspired. Once I brought my old school friend to visit her and even she left feeling the same way.

Some people just have that magic inside them. They wake you up to your own creativity.

"Freshwater View" (22 x 36, 2015). This was the view from the back path of the community I grew up in.

They transform you just by being in your presence. It has been a long time since I visited Gabby, but I still remember what she gave me: she showed me the wide-open space that was an artist's mind, and how I could surround my studio space with ideas. In her I could see the creative life as a real life in bits of paper, scraps of bank statements, and seashells and sand. Her gift was a lot more than that little wooden herring box that still hangs at the shore, but all the same, I am glad I have that souvenir. It reminds me that it was long ago but still so real. For that's what ideas and relationships are like: they are spirits in the wind, and sometimes you need something concrete—that bit of ephemera—to remind you that they really did exist.

"Chrysanthemum Sky" (48 x 52, 2018). This was hooked after a road trip to Advocate Harbour on the Bay of Fundy. Somewhere along the way, skies just became something for me to add decorative elements to. I love how these celestial flowers imply a kind of limitless spirit and mystery.

ONE OUT OF TEN

Every time we sell a kit in the studio there is a chance it will change someone's life. I know it sounds ridiculous. How could a rug-hooking kit change a life? But honest to goodness I believe it's true. And it is precisely because I believe it's true that I keep doing it.

Out of ten kits that sell in the studio, one or two might not get finished, but someone still learns the process. Six or seven will discover a new hobby and enjoy it for a long time. And maybe out of those ten, one will find that rug-hooking changes them. Just maybe, it will change their life. It might make them happier, or kinder, or help them see things differently. One of them will be changed because of that starter kit, and it is because of that one person that I feel I am making a difference. That one little soul finding its way in the world makes me feel like I am doing something worthwhile. It makes me feel like I am changing the world a little tiny bit at a time.

You see, for some people rug-hooking becomes a passion. For them, in doing it, they find a way to express themselves. Rug-hooking becomes their creative *tour de force*; they use it to learn about themselves, and to show the world who they are. All of a sudden they have more to say, and a way to say it beautifully. Through it they begin to see the world differently; the grass is no longer green, but shades of moss and tan and sage. The sky becomes bigger and in it they see shades of ecru and mauve and sometimes even butter yellow. The world becomes a place of beauty that is waiting to be translated into wool.

There is always that one anxious soul who is calmed by the motion of the hook slipping through the linen—that one person for whom the wool slipping through their fingers is a prayer. It connects them on a deeper level to the meaning that they seek. Maybe they feel closer to God through it, or maybe they achieve a kind of Zen.

I know this because I have found these things myself. When I don't hook for a little while I know there is something missing. My supposed "break" ends up becoming a bit of a test.

Years ago I used to take the month of December off. I remember putting my frame

"Across the Fence" (52 x 18, 2005). I grew up in a place like this and am grateful every day for that childhood of back paths, broken fences, neighbours who knew your name, and a sea to sit beside.

< "Spruce and Grey Skies" (10x 10, 2009). I love this raggedy grey and khaki combination with the green spruce trees. I have never found anything wrong with a grey day and a warm southeasterly wind.

"Visions of Spring" > (37 x 40, 2015). Elemental things, slightly morphed, like sunflowers, beach rocks, fish tails, and tulips are all thrown together in fresh spring colours. I love to hook shapes both well defined and slightly off kilter.

away to make room for the Christmas tree in mid-December one year. By Christmas Eve I was weepy for no good reason. Everything was irritating me and I felt lost. I remember breaking down in front of my sister-in-law. The shock on her face quickly faded to helplessness. *What in the world could I do with her*, read her face. I had no idea why I was crying. It was only after she left and I was alone that it dawned on me: I was missing my hook. I was missing that feeling of making something with my hands. All my creative energy was churning into something else and I was weeping instead of making. These were the early days of creativity for me. I never meant to be an artist—never set out to

be—this craft just fell upon me, and it made me an artist.

Over the twenty-five years I have taught people my craft, I learned that it has had the same effect for others. I have watched people become themselves through hooking rugs. It changed them, and it all started with a little pattern and a few strips of wool. There is so much more to making rugs than making rugs. I love the promise that the process holds for people, how it changes them and grows with them. It is such a beautiful thing to watch them bloom.

One in ten, maybe more, but it would be worth it no matter how many.

It is a beautiful thing.

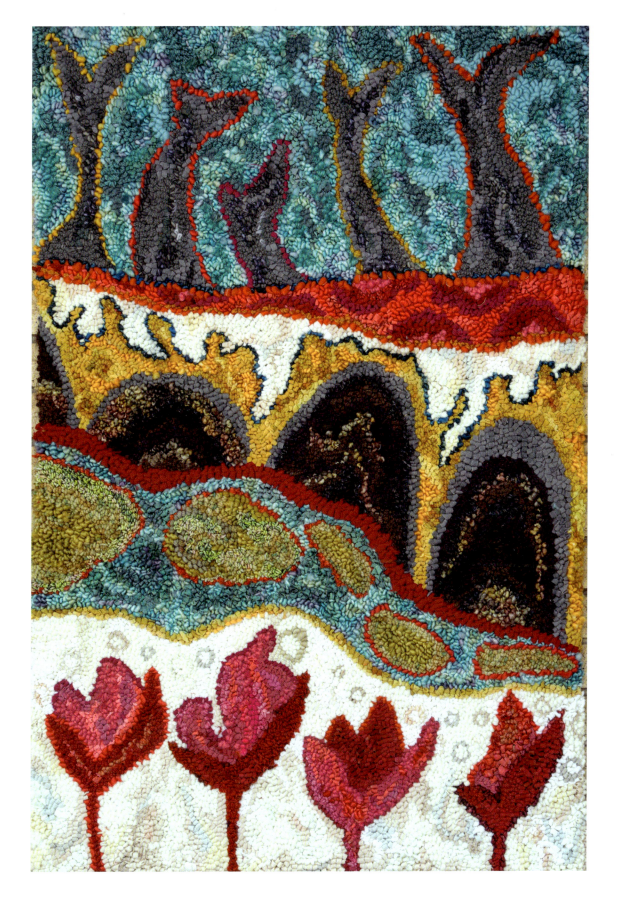

WAITING FOR THE MUSE

"**D**o you ever have a creative slump?" she asked me. I wanted to say, "No never." I wanted to lie like a thief, and I wanted the lie to be true.

I wanted to dance around and sing as if I were the wind, not just someone merely affected by it.

I wanted to avoid the truth. The truth that there is a natural part of making things that affects everyone sometimes: creative slumps are part of the making.

"Shut up and wait," I told her instead.

Because of course I have funks…I just wait them out. That's what you do when you are waiting for inspiration. There is no point going on and on about it. Instead you might as well make your bed, empty the garbage, or take a drive south (or north, or east, or even west). It does not matter what you do; just stop talking and thinking about the slump as if that will make a difference. Start *doing* something. Let go of your work for a little bit and just do other stuff. Visit people. Walk in different places. Go somewhere interesting. Pique your curiosity. Enjoy the time. Your work, no matter how important it is, is only a part of you. There is more to explore. When you are not busy being inspired, it is a great time to uncover other parts of yourself.

Some of you may ask: well, why shouldn't you talk about being stuck? Why shouldn't you mention the muse as if everybody knows her? Well, not talking about it too much is just my opinion. I am not an art therapist or even a regular therapist. I just don't think talking

"Love is a Storm" (22 x 40, 2017). This rug is the story of love in a marriage. The storybook idea that it just goes along happily is a myth. Good love that has any strength to it at all has weathered a storm or two.

about it helps. Being too focused on what you *don't* have makes you forget about what you *do* have. Then there is the fact that talking about inspiration and where it comes from and when and how it comes is boring for others. To hear someone drone on about not being inspired is terribly dull. It reminds me of talking about constipation, except not everyone can relate to not being inspired. It makes you sound like a parody of an artist instead of an artist.

You might tell someone that you've "got nothing" right now, but that's it. That's the limit right there. Move on to your dietary habits,

which are possibly more interesting. Talk about salmon fishing, or origami, or Batman. Just don't mention that you are stuck because it might lead you to get more stuck.

Just know this: inspiration comes in waves. Ride them. Ride them high and ride them low. When they are high, hold your head back and feel the breeze wash over you. Know the value of the ride, and be thankful for it. Keep a notepad nearby and sketch and write and document everything you can. Ride it like you are a great surfer. Ride it like you own it. When you are riding low, remember the big wave you just got off, be thankful for it, and know that another will swell soon. Get ready for the next one coming. Just bide your time and be thankful that there is a tide, and trust that it will come your way.

"Coral Cove" (10 x 14, 2018). The more I hook, the closer I look at painters like the Group of Seven for inspiration.

"Barn in the Field" (18 x 18, 2004) I live in a place full of barns, though they get fewer and fewer every year.

MAKER, MAKER

I hook all summer long. Once I have an idea, it does not matter the weather, I just want to hook it. I find it so soothing. The last couple of days I have been rushing around and feeling stressed. I know if I sit at the frame today that feeling will settle. It works for me. It is something that is as important to me in summer as it is in winter; it is without a season.

In fact, I sometimes resent the heat of the summer because it gets in the way of my hooking. When it is too hot to hook, I miss it. The feeling of wool slipping through my fingers is a tonic. Every time I walk toward my frame with a new idea it is like a beginning. Every time I emerge from the frame I feel a sense of release.

When I start a rug, I often have no idea where it is going—I'm just hopeful. It is a bit like establishing a new friendship; you ask a lot of questions of each other, and do lots of listening. You evaluate; take in the other. Sometimes one new idea leads to many more; other times, it is just the one.

Historically, women took charred pieces of wood from a fire to mark patterns on old burlap bags. They did this for beauty and function, but they also did it for solace. Women have made things with their hands for generations because it made them feel good to do so. They knew the benefits went beyond warming cold floors; they, like us, made things because it made them who they were and showed their lives.

It is an intuitive thing, this desire to create. It is in us from childhood, and probably more

"Make me a Channel of Your Peace" (36 x 42, 1997). I made this rug upon hearing about the death of Mother Theresa. I still say this prayer daily and just recently a friend gave me a quote from Mother Theresa to hang on my kitchen wall: "Do small things with great love." I think this is what hooking is.

alive and well in us then than when we are older. After all, who really *needs* a pair of home-knit socks anymore?

Well, I will tell you one person who does: the person who makes them. In the midst of raising children, or loving grandchildren, or tending house, or working a fancy job, there are times you need to pour your heart and love and mind into something tactile. Something you can watch grow gently beside you. Something that doesn't talk back or criticize. Something you can make. In a world where so much of our work has no tangible result, the domestic tasks of the handmade have a new and certain value. We need these tactile results more now than we ever did.

"Grace, Mercy, and Peace" (36 x 36, 1997). A portrait of my mother, this rug hangs over the tea kitchen at the studio. I see it every day and remember her.

"Turquoise Town" (13 x 45, 2016). This rug was about playing with shape and colour.

ON MAKING A LIFE

BECOMING YOURSELF

My son once said to me, "If you still had little kids running around, you would still be cranky." I knew there was truth in it, but it was not all true. I was a good mother, but I was not always a pleasant mother. I was warm and loving and I was cranky. In those days I still worked and ran a business, and tried to be a writer and an artist. I tried to do too much while my children were young. It was a mistake that I regret, but I also know that some kinds of wisdom come with age. Knowing that, I quickly forgive myself. How could I have known then what I know now?

But when I look back on it now, I wish I had had more patience. When my children were little I thought it was going to last forever—I was only twenty-seven when I had my son, and at that time I could never imagine him being an adult. It felt as if being a mom to young children was my new life, the one and only life I would ever know. I think most moms feel the same way. You think this new stage is now your life forever. I remember thinking this is the new me, the new us. I could not picture anything else because my son was so central to my life. When I had my second child, I was further in. Together, those two children were my reason for being. They needed me. Now we were a bigger family, and the only thing I could possibly foresee was nursery school.

Still, I worked on a business, and wrote, and made rugs, and tried to become an artist. I worked hard. Sometimes I would pack cards and make kits after the kids went to bed until late into the night.

It seems a lifetime ago. And it was, I guess. I wish I could have known how fast it was all going to go. It sped by, and I was present; I was aware of the time flying before my very eyes. I knew the value of the moment. But even being present, I was so immersed that it was hard to

< "One Hundred Acres" (52 x 44, 2010). I like to call this style of rug my "field rugs." They come from walking and watching the seasons change in the brush and scrub.

<< "Hold my Hand" (16 x 16, 2012). This was one of the illustrations for the children's book *Singily Skipping Along* by Sheree Fitch. We auctioned off all the rugs as a fundraiser for L'Arche Cape Breton.

"Watching Over"
(20 x 28, 2005). This rug
was commissioned by a
man for his wife as they
awaited the birth of their
first child.

picture a future where I would be fifty-two with two adult children. You cannot imagine that your little boy will be wearing a suit and tie. It is hard to think that little girl with the blunt bangs will be your friend.

Children changed my life; before them I was greedy about my time. They taught me how to sacrifice, and I don't think I would have ever learned it without them. But that is also why I was cranky when they were little—it's not like I transformed overnight. It was push and pull; a tug-of-war, in which they demanded and I learned to concede.

So my son is right: I might still be cranky if there were a bunch of kids running around, but I would also be better because *he* made me

better. It did not happen immediately but having children taught me to share my life. I learned that what I wanted sometimes did not matter one bit, and that I might as well get used to that feeling. I learned that helping someone come into themselves, helping them grow their own soul, was far more important than growing my own.

It was not easy, but when I look back I realize having children was not entirely about them after all. It was about me coming into myself, about me becoming softer, kinder…more of what I was supposed to be in the first place.

All along I thought I was nurturing their souls, but they were nurturing mine.

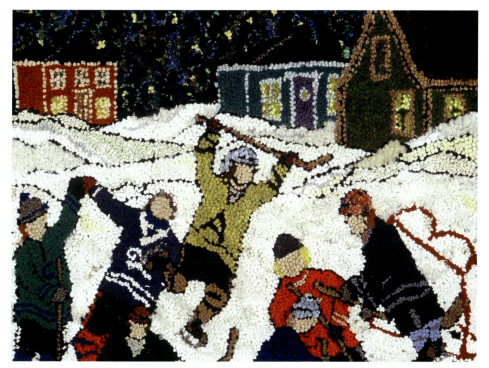

"Hockey Night in Nova Scotia" (30 x 36, 2001). This rug was made for my daughter, Adele, who played hockey. It was a big part of our lives.

"The Saltwater Dance" (28 x 36, 2003). This kind of rug grew out of a love for home and a romanticizing of Newfoundland. I did this a lot in my early rugs.

KEEP ON KEEPING ON

Today I walked by a house at the end of our road. Inside, I knew a woman was dying. After a long battle with cancer, she was coming to the end of her life. I noticed her lawn was perfectly mowed; manicured perfectly by her husband. I thought, "That's it, isn't it." Inside someone is at the end of her life, but outside the lawn still must be mowed. The world goes on around you, even as you are exiting it.

After a friend of mine died, her husband told me that when he found himself brushing his teeth, he knew he could go on. He would be sad but he could manage. Because the mundane must still be managed.

Outside, people are still going to restaurants. They are still raising glasses to toast each other. People are celebrating, sharing, making love, complaining, fighting, and doing all the things they always did even though you are saying goodbye to someone. It is shocking after you lose someone to watch the world go on as if nothing has happened. After a little while you find yourself a part of it, wondering how you fit in any longer. Wondering if you belong. You go through the motions of all the things that need to be done. Yet you are somehow distant from it, for your mind is elsewhere, and your heart is sinking. The mundane is necessary, and in times of loss, it can be a blessing. You fill the cup with tea though you can hardly taste it.

Loss, whether it is expected or sudden, whether it is the loss of a life, or a marriage, or a sudden change in circumstances, takes you aback. You are left uncertain about so much, feeling everything more deeply. It leaves you longing for love and connection.

Now that I am older, I have watched people leave this world and others come in to it fully. When my husband and I had our twenty-fifth anniversary party, we hired the same band that played at our wedding and celebrated in the same hall. You would think it would feel the same, but it did not. It was lovely but completely different. We were not beginning; we were solidly in the middle. Our aunts, uncles, and parents were no longer there to encourage us and push us on. There was a loneliness to it. We were now fully ourselves without the threads to home that our parents had provided for so long. Now *we* were the ties for a younger generation just emerging.

So there was also a joy for everything that had happened at the right time. Our adult children were there with us, their friends, their partners, dancing and smiling and shaking hands with our old friends. There was a new

"Intensity" (48 x 70, 2009). I wanted to work with reds and kept seeing this big carpet of red. The little bits of gold on the side shows my weakness for colour; I just had to add a little something.

"As For Me and My House" (48 x 54, 2009). This rug has a bible verse tucked in the bottom right corner: "As for me and my house, we will serve the Lord." For many years it was the first rug you saw when you entered my home; a reminder to myself to try and be good.

generation and we were the ones pushing them into the future.

All in good time, one generation replaced another, and none of those still here or those gone on would have it any other way.

We lose and gain so much as we age. Somehow we get used to death, and fear it less as so many of our family and friends have already done; it feels safer somehow. Those little children we nursed through colds and tantrums bloom into interesting people who add new ideas and new people to our lives. They keep us in touch with a new generation and add a little sparkle to our lives.

"Cold Winter Day" (40 x 48, 2008). I do not love winter, but I also do not have any desire to go south. I settle in with my hooking, my writing, and I make sure I have a good warm coat.

"Traditional Rose"
(13 inches, 2002).
My mother loved to
hook roses. When my
father described his
mother's rug-hooking,
he mentioned roses too.
This rose, for me, is an
emblem of my family
history in rug-hooking.

"Full Moon" (48 x 32, 2007). >
This rug makes me smile. I
wasn't there. It didn't happen.

ART IS A LOVE STORY

I fell in love with my husband because of a book. I fell in love with him because he had real paintings in a box underneath his couch. I fell in love with him because of art, and that was long before I knew I was an artist.

When I met this man in 1985—what seems now like a lifetime ago—I didn't know the difference between a picture and a painting. I had no love of the handmade. I knew nothing about art. I never imagined that people painted pictures for other people's walls. Art, as I thought of it, came from a store.

Two things changed within a week of meeting him. I was visiting his apartment around Christmastime and he had a tree set up. He had found it blowing across the parking lot when he came out of the hockey rink. It was a spindly thing and I don't remember any lights. I was lying on the carpeted floor playing records, and I asked him what was in the blue boxes under the couch. He pulled out the big film box, opened it, and showed me the paintings he had collected from an artist named Alfred Whitehead, who had taught in the music department at Mount Allison University.

I was astounded that he owned art. I had never met anyone who actually bought paintings. It was a completely new concept to me. At that moment, looking through that box of unframed oils and watercolours, I came to understand the difference between a picture and a painting.

Later that week I was looking through his bookcase. (I was as nosy then as I am now.) He did not have a lot of books but the ones he had I knew were good. I may have known nothing about art, but I knew books, even at twenty. He brought one down and handed it to me. It was a copy of David Adams Richards's *The Coming of Winter*. At the time I had never heard of him, but for years after he remained one of my favourite writers. He lent the book to me to read. More than the story itself, I remember reading it thinking, if a man likes a book like this then he is a good man.

I did not know it right then, but when I look back on it I realize I fell in love with my husband reading that book and looking at those paintings. Those two things brought me right to his heart and kept me there.

Art is like that; it is a love story. Over and over again people fall in love with paintings, books, music, and drama. Art allows us to connect with each other through creative expression, and we can love and find meaning in the same things. It stimulates our intellect, lays beauty before us, and stirs up emotion. I know that the book I found on my husband's shelf and the paintings he had under his couch showed me that we loved the same things and that because of that it would be easier to love each other. Art is like that; sometimes it leads you to love.

"Aunt Mary" and "Mr. Bernie" (14 x 49 each, 1996). Mary was my father's sister and she lived on the Southside Road in St. John's. Mr Bernie Dollimont was our next-door neighbour in Freshwater, and was a traditional Newfoundlander. These people loomed large in my childhood and gave me memories that will sustain me all my life.

"In My Yard" (20 x 34, 2009). These tiny paisleys in the sky and the raggedy spruce in the backfield feel like the land I live on. I still live on seven acres at the edge of town—the only home I have ever had in my adult life.

"Chapman Settlement" (70 x 18, 2005). I love the broad fields and plain white farmhouses along the Amherst Shore. It was walking along here that I first saw scrub and brush turn to wool and emerge in my mind as a rug.

NEWFOUNDLAND OR DISNEYLAND?

I never took my kids to Disneyland. It was a conscious decision, and I wondered as I was making it if I would regret it later. So many people we knew were going and enjoying it. It was *the* thing to do. It was a paradise for children, I knew, but I wanted my children to want something different. That was before I knew that your children would want what they wanted no matter want kind of parent you were.

Instead I took them to Newfoundland. As their tourism commercial said years later, Newfoundland is about as far from Disneyland as you can get. I had grown up on the island, but had only a few connections left there. All my sisters and our parents had long since moved to the mainland. I chose to take my kids there because I wanted them to know some of what I had known. I wanted them to know their own culture. It was a value-driven decision. I wanted them to feel Newfoundland more than Disneyland.

Values are funny things. When you make a decision based on your own set of values, it is as if you are being critical of others' choices. My friend used to say, "Well, you do kind of think what you choose is the best…if you didn't you wouldn't choose that, right?" Well, right, that's true. You make choices for you and your family because you think they are the best choices. You know it does not mean choices made by others are wrong, you just are choosing for yourself. Everyone is different, and that's okay, but the truth is: you think *your* choice is right.

When I look back I am so happy that I can picture my four-year-old boy sitting in the kitchen of a woman in Southeast Bight. I remember how happy he was to be given a whole package of strawberry wafer biscuits by

"Village" (58 x 28, 1996). I sent the Art Gallery of Nova Scotia snapshots of my rugs very early on. This one hung in my living room until the gallery called one afternoon and offered to buy it. I initially told them I did not want to sell it, but my husband eventually talked sense into me.

"The Fish are a-Jumping" (24 x 24, 2016). This rug was part of the "The Very Mention of Home" collection I created to explore the nature of our relationship with the notion of home. Since fish and fishing were such a huge part of my childhood, they figure largely in these pieces.

a woman neither of us knew. I loved seeing my kids stand in doorways, water rolling by behind them. There were long drives to nowhere, visits in kitchens, and tea and raisin buns. There were flat-top houses, boat rides, and small gifts from strangers. It wasn't much, really, but to me it was important.

And I have never regretted that choice. My children can go to Disneyland now if they want. When they have kids they can take their own babies there if they want. Me, I wanted something different for them. I chose something plainer and simpler. I wanted to give them a little taste of what I knew; I wanted them to see what influenced my work; I wanted to give them a little bit of myself. I wanted to share the land I knew more than I wanted to share a fantasy land. I am not sure they cared much either way. They were happy to pack the car and head off in any direction for a family vacation. You cannot give your children everything; sometimes you have to just give them what you think is important.

So I did that. No regrets.

"Big Hills in the Narrows" (54 x 17, 2014). This rug was inspired by a trip to Paradise, Placentia Bay, I took with my Uncle Donald when I was fifteen.

"Chapman Settlement #2" (70 x 18, 2005). Another view from my long walks at Amherst Shore. Walking helped establish me as an artist; a time to think of and work through ideas.

WE KNOW IT WHEN WE SEE IT

They say there are only a few good stories in the world, so I am always a bit surprised when my rugs really resonate with someone from a completely different background.

Sometimes, when they look at my rugs, they see a completely different story from the one I thought I was hooking. Their ideas about my work come from their experience, and provide their own context. That is why art is universal. We all look at the same thing and take away something different.

At first I was very interested in the narrative aspect of rug-hooking and was anxious to tell people the stories behind my mats. But that quickly changed. To me, it became more interesting to hear what the viewer saw in the rugs. Sometimes I even learned things about the work—or about myself—through their eyes. It was interesting. It turned out I was sometimes working at a subconscious level; things would come out that I knew were inside of me but that I was not necessarily setting out to show.

Once I was working on a portrait of a woman in front of the hills at Argentia. She was standing alone, and there was a lot of water in the background. Another artist walked in the studio and asked about the paisley pattern I was hooking into the water. I said I didn't know—because I didn't. I was just working intuitively, creating beauty, the best way I knew how. She

"Lavender and Rain 1" (20x 20, 2010). Sometimes my rugs are somewhere between abstract and landscape. I especially love how the sky morphed into birch trees.

"An Ocean of Tears" (40 x 58, 2008). The paisleys showed up in the ocean as I was hooking it and an artist friend came in and said "It looks like an ocean of tears." I feel this rug is a lament for having left Newfoundland and having stayed away.

looked at me and said, "It's almost like an ocean of tears."

Then it dawned on me: I was making a self-portrait. This woman was me, leaving Argentia at sixteen, lonely. I am a proud Newfoundlander, to the point that I am almost righteous about it. Growing up there shaped me, and made me so much of what I am. I am never embarrassed of my accent, or uncomfortable that I grew up in a tiny place in a plain house with working-class people. I love the idea of it—it is me.

It's so much a part of me that for years I struggled to reconcile with leaving Newfoundland. I always planned to go back and live there. When I did eventually go back for university, I left after two years of study and returned to

"Between Two Places" (36 x 36, 2016). This is the story of my art and my life. It has been spent between Nova Scotia and Newfoundland. I am grounded in both places, love them equally, and belong in either.

Nova Scotia. Newfoundland was a critical part of me, but not so much that I wanted to stay. I was happy leaving; I was ready when I left the second time. And I have always been a bit torn by that.

In leaving that rocky outcrop, I left not only a place but also a culture—and for years it was a struggle for me. I have often felt, and still do, that I left something critical behind. I am still a Newfoundlander, but I am not there. That is what came out in the rug with the paisley sea.

Sometimes you can hook a story that is more than you know, and that is the beauty of art.

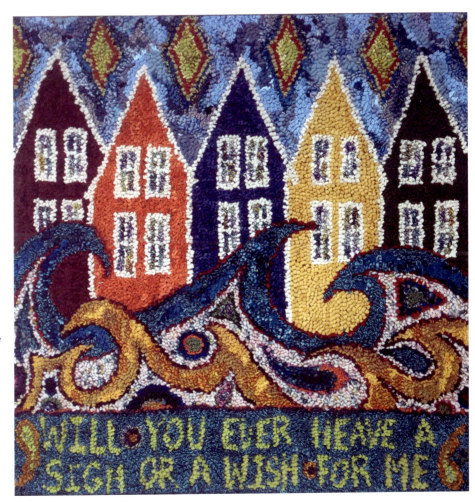

"Will You Ever" (36 x 36, 2016). I rarely travel south, but I was walking on a beach in Cuba and watching the big waves roll ashore when I thought of home. Whenever I travel, I miss this rugged landscape no matter how beautiful it is where I go.

ENOUGH

Y ou cannot be everything all at once.
You are what you are.
Beauty is on the inside.
We all know these mantras. We have heard them a hundred times. Yet we often find ourselves wondering, "Am I enough?" Whether or not we've thought those exact words, we would not be saying, "I need to lose ten pounds" or comparing ourselves to others if we were sure we were enough.

Recently I was surprised when a few of my friends and I all agreed that sometimes we felt not enough. We talked about it, and owned it. It was not that people made us feel that way, we just *were* that way.

A few years ago there was a trend online where people wrote, "I am enough" somewhere on themselves and had their picture taken. I liked this trend; it is good to reinforce the idea that you are enough. Then I started to feel that old familiar gnawing: "If *she* is enough, how come sometimes I don't feel like enough?" My friends and I were honest with each other:

sometimes we compare ourselves with others, and sometimes we feel that we are not enough—not good enough, not loving enough, not kind enough, not thin enough.

Lately I have been hearing women say, "Oh, I'm past all that." And some are, I am sure. But some, I am also sure, are not. Some are past it some of the time. Some struggle with it occasionally.

Some days I am enough—some days I am *more* than enough—but frankly, some days I could do better. Some days I could be kinder, more generous. Maybe I returned home with kitchen envy. Maybe I ate a big pistachio square at the local deli. Maybe I snapped at my husband. Maybe I looked at the beautiful people across the room and felt frumpy. Maybe I did not do any of those things in the last week, but I know I am susceptible and I know they might happen again.

Because sometimes I am good, and sometimes I feel I'm a bit…well, you know…a bit "not good enough."

I just want to say that this struggle seems real to a lot of us.

"Mermaids at Midnight" (54 x 18, 2004). Pure playfulness and joy; I let that into my rugs as much as I can.

"Comparison is the thief of joy" said Theodore Roosevelt, and that was before Instagram, Facebook, and photographic filters. That was before social media—where no one ever posts that they just picked their nose. (Warning: if you are thinking of posting that just to "even things out a little," don't. It is just not something we need to know.) The thing is, comparing ourselves to others might rob us of joy, but it can also be helpful. It might make us strive to be a little kinder, a little healthier, a little better. Only a rare few of us have been blessed with the kind of self-possession that keeps us from looking at what the other fella is doing. If you have it, well, good for you. Honestly, that is great. But for the rest of us, we are only human, and sometimes we might forget our blessings.

We have been given hearts to love and minds to think, so it is natural to wonder. And sometimes we might even wonder about ourselves.

"Women and the Sea" (20 x 26, 2015). I teach classes online and this was a pattern I created just for that. I love the idea of women in red coats guarding the coast; a kind of metaphor for the Mounties.

KIN

It was a little holiday we were having, sitting around eating squares and drinking tea on a sunny summer day. His cellphone rang. "Don't answer it," his wife said firmly.

He answered it.

She shook her head. "I leave mine in the car. He does not need it." Then she looked at me and said, "He needs to be needed."

And, actually, I understood. For her husband was my kin and I, too, need to be needed. I had thought about this before, but suddenly there it was laid out in front of me: it's not just me! It probably has to do with the blood we share. We like to help other people, but we also like what we ourselves get from doing that. It feeds something in us. We check our phones because we like being wanted. It reassures us. His wife

and a million other people like her do not need that validation and are comfortable in their own skin. My kind and I just feel a bit cozier and a bit more loved when we are needed.

It was an off-hand comment she made over a cup of tea at the kitchen table and my cousin wasn't bothered by it, but sometimes those quick statements resonate, and that day it resonated with me.

This slightly greedy desire to be needed is a Fitzpatrick trait, I think. I remember my father being just like this. We are all happy to help where we can—we even want to help—but part of the want is because it feeds something in us. We like to be involved.

I would say his wife is right, but it is not just him; we all need to be needed.

I think about the generation before us: Andy, Mary, Bill, and Donald. They were all like that. They all had people that they were good to, that they checked on, that they buoyed. It was their nature, and because it was, it is now our nature. My sisters and cousins, I see it in all of them. We are people who love, because it comes back tenfold.

Mostly, though, the comment made me think about this need within myself, and in a way it helped me feel a bit more comfortable with it. I know I have this uncontrollable need, but now I feel less alone with it. It is not just me, and it is not some kind of weakness; it's a family trait. It is just kin…we're like that.

"Under the Quilts" (38 inches, 1999). There were times in my childhood when everyone was home and we were three or four to a bed. I remember being tangled up in my mother's heavy lumpy quilts made from my sisters' old clothes.

"Lavender and Rain 2" (20 x 20, 2010).

THE LITTLE COTTAGE

We had just come back from a vacation in the Gaspé with our nine-month-old son. It was a beautiful place, but our son cried the whole way there. We ended up staying in a dull motel room with a red polyester bedspread. It was a long five days, and one of those road trips that makes you wonder why you are on the road at all.

We came home tired and irritated and went to visit my husband's parents at Amherst Shore, which led us to the little cottage. After our trip to the Gaspé we arrived at Amherst Shore and thought, "Why weren't we here? Why did we drive over six hundred kilometres for a polyester bedspread? Look what we left behind!" The Northumberland Strait was spread out before us like a blanket. That sea of undiscovered peace was there, just waiting for us to sit down beside it and be quiet.

The cottage itself, well, that was another matter; it was a junk shed, really. My in-laws stored an old boat in there that had not seen water in thirty years, and there were a couple of spring beds. The little cottage was covered in varnished plywood, and there were a couple of old wooden tables inside and a few bits of mismatched furniture. A few walls were painted light blue by someone who had tried to resurrect it twenty years before. There was running water, which was cold and ran right underneath the cottage. Behind the cottage was a traditional outhouse with a shed roof.

I spent several summers in that little green cottage; it was no palace but it was a kind of paradise. All we needed was a place to lay our heads and the little cottage gave us that. It was like we belonged there now that we had a child of our own. My husband had grown up on that very beach, and I had grown up on a much rougher, craggier shore; we were happy to be by the ocean again. Sandy or rocky, I wanted my child to have the sea. It is so much to give someone, a childhood by the sea. I knew that then, and I still believe it now. It is a gift that would live in them as long as forever.

Summers were slow there; I would sit on the deck and hook rugs every day. My son would crawl around on the deck beside me. I watched him closely—one eye on my rug and one on him—making sure he did not crawl out between the palings. I nailed a little piece of wood to the bottom of the screen door so he could go in and out of the cottage on his own. That little

"Hanging the Wash" (8 x 32, 1998). This early rug, with all its sweetness, looks so simple to me now. I love that I have a record of where I was and what I did.

homemade doorknob was his first taste of independence, and for years it served as a reminder to me about how time passes. My in-laws were next door so there was always help around.

Really all we had in that place was a roof over our heads, but there was so much more to it for us. The feeling that you could sit by the sea and hear the tide coming and going was so comforting and reassuring. All of a sudden the feeling that our son would soon be able to run next door to his grandparents' on his own seemed so lovely.

Until he came along we had spent very little time there, but he helped us see what we had. He helped us understand that what we had once been given ourselves was important to share again. For us, being by the sea was like being home. Children do that: they bring you home.

"Beach Path" (54 x 32, 2014). There is a little tidal pool at "the point" on the Amherst Shore, often filled with navy blue starfish. I love the mystery in the shape and form of seaweed and barnacles. I cannot imagine I will ever tire of it.

"Wildflowers" (36 x 54 , 2000). I saw a crow coming up out of the ditch one morning and when I drew it, the wildflowers appeared. I love the words in this rug and its variety of colours; it remains beautiful to me years after it was made.

"Women Working" (48 x 16, 2007). > This rug is inspired by my mother's work ethic and the old Sobeys uniforms of the 1990s. Odd combination, I know, but true. That's art; odd things come together.

THE GOOD IN PEOPLE

We were driving up the lane from the shore when a neighbour stopped our car. My husband rolled down the window and I leaned over him to listen.

"I just wanted to tell you that I noticed what you did," she said.

She thanked us for something that, in most cases, would go unnoticed—or at least unremarked. She had seen us being kind to someone who can be a pain in the arse. She said she liked to let people know when they had done something good. We laughed, but honestly we appreciated it, because it is nice to be thanked, to be considered.

I like to imagine what it would be like if we all took that approach with each other. What if, instead of judging, we picked apart the good in people? I should try that instead of dwelling on the littlest things someone has done to irritate me. It is so easy to fall into the habit of focusing on the faults of others. When someone does something that bugs me, I magnify it for a while; hold it tight to my chest (and against them) a bit, until I come to my senses. I carry these slights around like tiny weights in my pockets, until one day I pull them out and toss them aside.

It is not easy to forgive each other our small injustices. We have a habit of slighting each other in ways we don't even notice until *we* are the ones slighted. I can think of a thousand times I have said no to an invitation, never imagining that I might be hurting someone's feelings in doing so. I probably have.

As I have aged, all these little things—these tiny slights—bother me less. I surrender them more quickly, though I still lack enough wisdom to not let them bother me in the first place. These days, I don't want any extra weight on—no balls and chains. I do not want to feel the need to avoid anyone. I want to mend things, create things, and inspire others to be better, stronger. The only way I can do that is to be better myself. I want to act like an elder might. I want to actually be wise, not just say the words I imagine wisdom might speak.

Actually, my marriage has helped with this. In any good marriage, both partners become more themselves because they have the other person to provide some extra buoyancy. I have always counted on my husband to help me see the other side of an argument. We stay afloat because someone is giving us that extra push.

We sail because they give us room. He tells me when I am off course and helps me find my way; I do the same for him.

A friendship is much the same. Sometimes you have to whisper a confidence so that you can weigh both sides with someone who understands. A good friend can pull you back from anger, and help you forget the little things you feel irritated about. Humans live in communities because we need each other. We thrive because we are good to each other; holding small slights close to your chest does not build community, it tears it down. So this week I will try to remember to pick apart the good in people.

One day a friend was listening to one community member complain about another. He came to the other's defence, saying, "I like them. I find them all right."

The person complaining dismissed this, saying, "You love everybody."

My friend responded, "Maybe, but it isn't easy."

I loved that response. It reminded me of my neighbour's desire to pick apart and acknowledge the good in people.

Nurture.

Sow.

Mend.

Make.

Find the good in people.

"Under a Cream Sky" (15 x 20, 2015). Remembering that the sky is not always blue and grass is not always green is important as an artist.

"Red Leaves at the Sea" (57 x 57, 2015). I like to layer landscapes using big natural motifs like the leaves, but I also used a triangular house motif in the uppermost hills. I have always liked how the middle hills resemble birds.

THE STORIES WE TELL

Whenever my cousin Donnie comes to visit he reminds me that he believes our grandfather's brother burnt down St. John's. According to the records, there actually was a Tom Fitzpatrick who accidentally dropped a spark into a hay barn in 1892, which grew into a fire that levelled St. John's. My cousin believes it was a relative because he said our grandfather turned up in Paradise alone shortly after the fire. He believes our grandfather was escaping a lot of hard feelings that were held against one Tom Fitzpatrick and all his family. It is true that all the other members of our grandfather's family left St. John's as well, eventually settling in the States or elsewhere. We never really knew how or why our grandfather ended up in Paradise, but it is so much more interesting to think that he was escaping blame for the Great Fire than to think he went fishing.

Donnie has done a little research in the local archives and has only come up with the fact that there were two men named Tom Fitzpatrick in St. John's at that time, and we were related to one of them. Which one? I still wonder. Is our family really part of that bigger story? In July 1892, eleven thousand people were left homeless and there was $13 million in property damage because Tom Fitzpatrick dropped a pipe or a match in the hay. Why is there some part of me that would like it to be true that he was our relative? Isn't it odd that we want to identify with someone who caused so much trouble for so many people?

When I asked my cousin, doubting the likelihood of this family history, he said there was no way to know. The records were, of course, all burned. We may or may not be related to "that" Tom Fitzpatrick.

"Coming Down From the Mountain" (44 x 51, 2004). I hooked this rug after I took a long hike to the top of Economy Mountain. Interestingly, I eventually took the figure out of the rug and just made it a landscape.

"Floating in Paradise" (36 x 36, 2016). Here I make reference to my father's childhood home of Paradise, which was part of the Newfoundland resettlement program. There is also a reference to those people who floated their houses across the bay.

This whole debacle reminds me of my father, who used to claim our family were once pirates off the coast of Newfoundland. As a child I had no idea this was common folklore in so many families. I loved the story and my father told it like it was fact. He had a penchant for storytelling, and was a great believer that the best part of any story was not necessarily the truth.

I just find it interesting how much we love a scoundrel in our past. We like to hear about those rogues and robbers that came before us and spawned our great-great-somebody. It makes us so much more colourful now that we are past all that.

Yet when we have one in the family in the present day, they drive us crazy. The loud drinkers, the petty thieves, the careless fools are almost intolerable in the present sometimes. We love them, but they wear us right out. You need some distance from them, but there is no getting it. It takes generations to give us the distance we need. It is interesting to think that this generation's "troubled soul" might become the legend of the family in the future.

Who would've ever guessed?

"Woman in a Blue Dress" (30 x 50, 2005). As a little girl I watched all my older sisters becoming women, dating and marrying. Watching women, how they dress, how they move, has always been interesting for me.

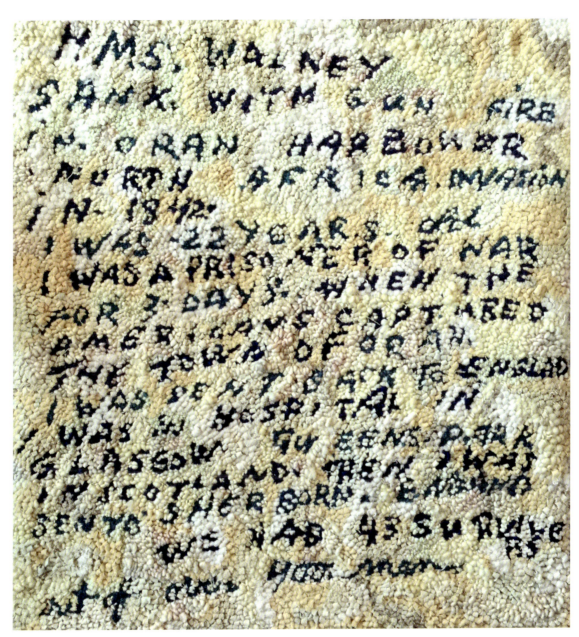

"War Story" (27 x 29, 2014). My uncle Donald Fitzpatrick was in the British Navy in the Second World War and his ship was bombed. He was one of just forty-three survivors out of over four hundred. One day we were driving and he wrote the story in my sketchbook. It was the only time he ever talked about it with me. I transposed his words onto linen and hooked it after he died.

EVERYDAY FAIRY TALES

Sometimes my daughter calls or texts me wondering about relationships. I want to tell her that your life with someone should be a love story, but I don't. Because that sounds so different than it really is. Telling someone relationships should be love stories puts a lot of pressure on both parties and makes it sound like everything should be glamorous, passionate, and exciting.

The foundation of fairy-tale love stories is a relationship that is solid forever. It is the traditional happily ever after. But a real love story is so much more than that—a real love story weaves itself through thick and thin. A love story is just about belonging to each other for a very long time.

I know of love stories where one person died, and the other lived fifteen more years missing them. I know of love stories where one person waited while the other had affair after affair. I know of love stories where one person was away for more than half their married life. There are love stories where one person loved drinking, and the other person loved the one who drank. These are the real love stories. They are muddied and complicated. They are sad and tragic, and at

"The Boy From Point Verde" (12 x 20 each, 2007). My friend Earl McGrath used to come to Freshwater to visit when I was a teenager. He still drops by in Amherst if he is passing through. There is something lovely about the friendships with people who have known you all your life; there's no room for pretense.

the same time they are beautiful…because they are still love stories.

Then there are the less complicated love stories where the couple just ate supper together and watched television every night for thirty years. There are love stories where each person was patient and kind and thoughtful, or brought the other tea in the morning.

I cannot tell my twenty-year-old daughter that any of these is a love story; I don't want to make her jaded or cynical. I cannot tell her that in some love stories people are bored, but they still love. But she will understand when she writes her own love story.

I have lived a love story simply by virtue of having a long marriage. Whatever has happened in those twenty-five-plus years we have been married doesn't need to be recounted here to prove ours is a love story. Love stories just happen when you stay together for a long time. That is marvellous in itself, the staying together. It is the deepest kind of river that can run between two people, that river of time. It is the kind of thing you understand because you experience it.

I remember asking my mother once if she loved my father. She replied, "Deanne, what is love?"

For years I felt that this was such a harsh answer. I was young, and I wanted to know if she loved him. Now I look back on it and I see that the answer was never in her words. It would never have mattered what she said. It was what she did. She lived with her husband, my father, for over forty years. She remained married to him until he died. It, too, was a love story, no matter what happened in the intervening years; it was a love story because they remained together through it all.

Love stories are not fairy tales; they are real people falling into each other's arms time and time again, forgiving what has happened between them, and trying hard to be good to each other.

"Fish Houses on the Coast" (24 x 58, 2006). I grew up around hills like this that buffered the Atlantic Ocean. They are in me. I love to hook them. I never tire of it because they take me home.

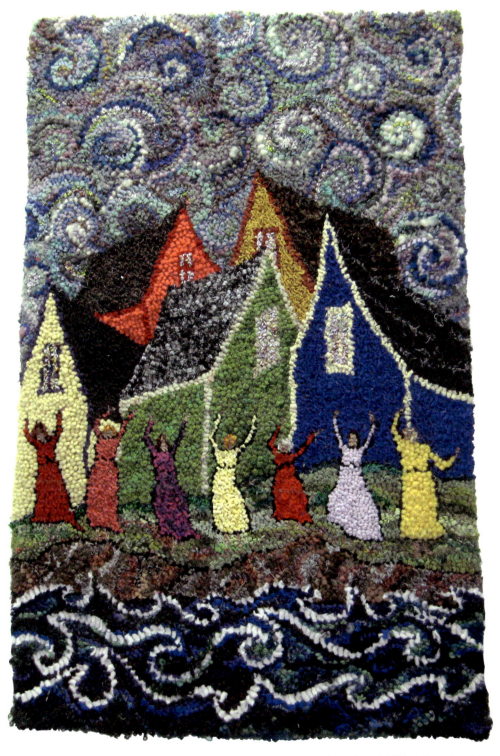

"Women by the Sea" (34 x 56, 2005). Seven women appear again and again! When I was hooking this rug I was thinking a lot about the colour relationship between the dresses and the houses.

ACCORDION DREAMS

Afamiliar tune will take you home; its sweet song will carry you back years and years, across a thousand miles, and set you somewhere you used to be.

This is exactly what happened to me one morning as I walked down the beach at Amherst Shore. The sandy coast is always littered with moon snails and razorfish, and occasionally the sun glints off a tiny piece of sea glass underfoot. It's a different shore than the rocky, black-and-grey coast I grew up on, but that morning in Amherst I felt like I was walking up and down the hills of Placentia Bay—the sound that was

swirling out onto the sea from a cottage above me was pure Newfoundland.

A woman was playing a familiar tune on the accordion, perched on the bank above the sand where I was walking. I couldn't tell you the name of the song, but I know I've heard it plenty of times before. I was completely transported, carried off to another time and place.

Suddenly I was a child, standing outside the church hall as wedding festivities were going on. I paused to admire the pink-and-white tissue-paper flowers on the big, baby blue sedans that carried the wedding party. How I loved seeing wedding processions when I was a child: the cars covered in papery flowers parading by, trying to get a glimpse of the bride in the back

"Mummers on a Starry Night" (70 x 72, 1997). Mummering is unique to Newfoundland, though many artists have explored it. I have only one vague memory of it happening in our home as it had gone out of fashion where I lived.

seat. So little happened where I lived, weddings were like a festival. Streamers and long polyester dresses made it feel like there was something magical happening. I can see it now, a church set against the backdrop of the bay.

It was magical after all.

Being ready for inspiration to hit you is about so much more than simply seeing; it is about paying attention to all your senses, and being ready, when the moment hits, to make a note of it in your mind. And yes, sound can be the muse. It can create the rhythm for your hooking. It can be the subject, or it can be the force behind it. It is the spark for so many memories.

Hearing that accordion along the Amherst Shore also reminded me of when I thought traditional music was old-fashioned. Maybe I was ten or twelve, and I remember thinking "old music" was a bit foolish. Good for a dance on

the Cape Shore, maybe, but not modern enough for my taste. I shunned it for a while, even felt embarrassed by it in my early teens.

A man by the name of Mr. Pete Barron cured me of that one evening when I was about sixteen. While I was waiting for his daughter to come out around the track to help me drink a six-pack of Black Horse beer, he came out with his accordion. He was a small man and when he stretched the black, red, and white accordion it appeared to be as big as him. He played "The Wild Colonial Boy" for me in his kitchen, in a little bungalow by the brook, and I began to cry. My mother used to sing that song around our kitchen when I was little. His playing brought back something I had lost, and the comfort in it brought me to tears. Suddenly the accordion was okay again. I never shunned traditional music after that…I just let it take me home.

"Pink Foxes" (45 x 31, 2017). My mother used to use the expression "as cute as a fox," meaning the person was a bit sly or had ulterior motives. I love the fox silhouette and how it sort of sneaks in.

"Layers of the Lake" (44 x 66, 2015). In this layered landscape, I was imagining what lay under the surface of the lake and exploring movement in my hooking. I love the sailors' warning in the red sky contrasted with the blues and turquoises.

THE POWER OF HANDWORK

O ver the years I have taught many people to hook rugs. When I teach, I know some people will become transformed. For some of them, rug-hooking will change their lives completely. It's hard to imagine a little craft project could do that, but I can usually feel it with people right away. The act of pulling wool through linen deepens their connection with themselves almost immediately. It's tangible. They feel as if they belong to it. Other times it may take a project or two before they feel the potential it can bring. I love seeing this.

I always feel, though, that when someone commits him- or herself to a craft and they practice it regularly, something bigger and more important happens. I have watched rug-hooking change people, so when I teach I know there is potential for real and beautiful change.

Creativity and handwork add layers to your life. It's not just the tactile thing you make, but also the self-understanding, creative expression, and the connections you can establish with yourself and others. We have underestimated its power for generations, but that time is gone. It is no longer "women's work," and it is no longer even just handwork: it is now mind work. To me, rug-hooking is close to meditation—you have a thrumming rhythm that is your mantra, you get lost in thought until the thoughts just go, and you reach a level (or place) where you are just in the moment. The meditative qualities of rug-hooking soothe us, and at times even console us.

It also builds community. Through it, we embrace each other in deep and lasting friendships. We learn that in supporting each other we simultaneously nurture ourselves—that in giving, we are so much more likely to receive. Friendship is so valuable to our personal evolution as human beings; through it we become softer and stronger at the same time.

We also learn that with our own hands we can create art. Art for our homes, for our friends, and sometimes even for our communities. And this is no small thing. Art brings beauty into the world and beauty transforms the

"Posy Pot Hit and Miss" (48 x 10, 1999). This is the kind of design I would draw for my mother when she started hooking rugs again in her seventies. She had not hooked since she was five, and began again making mats similar to the ones she had hooked with her mother when she was a child.

world. In times of heady discussion and political discourse, I often retreat to my rug-hooking frame because it is there that I can really add something to the world—albeit in a small way—and to me it remains meaningful. When people are talking away about things I cannot bear to hear, I retreat to art. It is what I can deal with, and it is what matters to me.

Making things adds to our quality of life. I honestly can say I do not know who I would be or what I would be like without the freedom of expression rug-hooking has given me. It has changed me and in doing that, it changed the world around me. I have watched it do the same for so many people, so I know rug-hooking is powerful work. That little bit of hand-over-hand softens things just a little, keeping your mind in the moment.

"The River in Winter" (32 x 10, 2018). This is part of a series I go back to again and again. I love looking at land topographically. It completely changes my view and I see the richness of shape and form from a new angle.

"Organic Garden" (35 x 22, 2013). The longer I hook, the less important image becomes and the more I value colour and form.

CONCLUSION

I feel both lucky and blessed to have found rug-hooking and to have learned early that it is so much more than making mats for old houses. I learned quickly that it was a means of expression, an art form. It has given me the chance to speak without ever saying a word. It has allowed me opportunities I never would've known possible. It has built a community for me, and a business, and it helped me make a life I love.

Hooking rugs continues to be the thing I love to do with my time—that has not changed in all these years. It has defined me both as an artist and as a human being. I am ever grateful for the blessing it has been and continues to be in my life.

Hooking rugs is an art form and art never ends; it lives within you, and the spirit of your ideas outlives you. Ideas can become more alive as they are mixed and blended with other ideas. They change and grow and become something beyond you. Once you let an idea out there, it becomes something different—and sometimes something bigger—than what you started. That's just how it is. No matter how protective you are with your thoughts and your creative work, once you show it, a new life begins.

I have let a lot of ideas out there. I make rugs because I have to, because I am compelled to. Just like I was when I started. I sit with the hook so I can create a bit of beauty. I like the way one loop leads to another, how the wools blend together to create something where once there was nothing.

Writing this book and recollecting all the rugs I have made in the past twenty-five years has reminded me of what I have done, how far I have come, and where I have yet to go. I am still an artist who will keep making rugs that are unmistakably art. Seeing beauty emerge from your own hands, inspired by your own thoughts and ideas, makes life better, kinder, and softer. I cannot imagine a life without making, or without creativity. These things are embedded in my soul, are part of my being. When I hook rugs I feel like I am getting back to myself, and back to what matters.

It has been a blessing.

"Crows and Acanthus Leaves" (72 x 50, 2010). I made this for my own floor, but eventually gave it to one of my sisters. She, in turn, gave it to Georgina Sicheri, who worked with me for a few years. It is now on her floor. I still like the idea of making mats for the floor. I love the utility of rug-hooking, and feel it can serve us as well on the floor as on the wall.

"The Virtuous Wife" (48 x 60, 2000). I love how this story in Proverbs reminds us that women have been in business forever, using it to care for the people around them and their families.

ACKNOWLEDGEMENTS

I am endlessly thankful for my husband, Robert Mansour. Living with an artist—whose mind is often more on the mat she is working on than the details of her life—takes kindness and patience. My children, Mikhial and Adele, suffer the same fate. This little family we have together is a beautiful thing and every day I am grateful. Thank you, you are all a blessing.

Lorna Davis looks after so many details of my life. Georgina, Angie, Mary, Logan, Greg, Angela, and Brenda, who work with me daily at my studio, are smart, kind, patient people.

Thank you to Nimbus Publishing and the people who work there. You have made it possible for me to write six books and be published close to home. As a regional publisher you are building our culture in Atlantic Canada and allowing us to express our unique reality. This is more important now than ever. Emily MacKinnon at Nimbus made this book so much better with her edits and helped give it the structure it needed.

Thank you. Each of you.

"New Country Moon" (37 x 15, 2015). This is the landscape that is all around me. The blueberry fields of Cumberland County have replaced the dark rocks of Newfoundland, and now I love them too.